We've Got to **START** Meeting Like This!

Edited by Michelle Auerbach
Cover designed in collaboration between
Nate Tanemori, Marianne Rodgers and Emily Shepard
Layout by Julia Restin
Author photo by Deidre Fuller

ISBN-10: 0615881181
ISBN-13: 978-0615881188

 **Raves**

"Brilliant! From Meetup.com to Lightning Talks, Dana stitches all the hot event trends into a cohesive story. A must have for any facilitator's bookshelf."

— **Jesse Fewell**
Agile Management writer, speaker, trainer

"Dana is absolutely the perfect person to take this on. She's had an insider's view of the good, the bad, and the ugly of many conferences/meetings. If anyone can break down how they OUGHT to be done, Dana is the one.

Want your conference or seminar to stand out among the pack of meetings your customers and prospects attend every year? Then you MUST read this book. Dana has captured the essential elements to help you bring the absolute best experience to your group. She's drawn rich content from a collection of experts in this field to complement her own methodology. And she's wisely organized her book so you can put it to use right away!"

— **Steve Ciesinski**
Vice President and General Manager, SRI International

"Dana Wright imagined all aspects of creating and implementing a conference in a way that enabled me to visualize what such events will be like. She's reached out to many others for ideas. She's drawn on her experiences, both as a conference attendee and as a Graphic Facilitator. She shows up and as she works she observes—as Yogi Berra said, 'You observe a lot by watching.'

And, when you read this book you'll experience what *can* be—as we START Meeting Like This. Get, read, and re-read this book. Demand that the conferences you attend are worthy of you, your time, and your attention. Together we can change the world of conferences."

— **Geoff Ball**
President, Smart Groups®

"Do you want your conference, meeting, or event to be inspiring? Dana has really captured a winning formula to engage the delegate before, during, and after an event; with this approach meetings will never be the same! I would strongly recommend this book to anyone who wishes to create a truly engaging experience!"

— **Patrick Marr**
Managing Director, Leading Edge

"Most people agree that meetings are corporate rituals that rarely achieve their desired impact. *We've Got to START Meeting Like This* is chock full of cutting-edge techniques to turn a mundane meeting into a truly transformative experience. Read it and pick up practical and pioneering practices that will make your next meeting, offsite, or event an irrefutable home run!"

— **Jessica Amortegui**
Director Global Talent Development, VMware

"For change practitioners, meetings can be powerful events to help shift behaviors and generate momentum. Dana has provided a simple framework for thinking through meetings and compiled a list of creative ideas for making these gatherings more effective."

— **Vivian Li**
Change Implementation Consultant, Expressworks

INTRODUCTION

"There is a book inside all of us."

I was returning home from a meeting in Chicago when this book was conceived—I had an urge to write down just a few thoughts. When I landed, I realized I had outlined an entire book. Later, I shared the outline with my friend Kathy, who thought it was a great idea. The more people I shared the concept with, the more delighted I became—everyone thought it was a book that was so needed and after all the hundreds of meetings I've facilitated or provided graphic recording, I was a great person to channel it.

As I worked on this, I realized that there was an underpinning concept that was the basis for the ideas. One evening at a restaurant, as I waited for my food to arrive, I sketched out the basic elements that became the START Meeting Model.

"Write the book you'd want to read."

With every step of writing this book, I gathered information from friends and colleagues who saw meetings the way I did. I have become more and more excited about the concepts that were shared with me. Connecting them together energized me to gather more. I reached out to close friends and then networked, using social media, with colleagues around the world. I was always delighted when people agreed to let me work with their terrific ideas for creating engagement and sharing knowledge.

This book is not targeted at a small audience. There are pieces that meeting and event planners will really relate to. There are parts that will be useful for meeting facilitators as well as graphic recorders. There are sections that are very useful for presenters and speakers. And, there are lots of great ideas for meeting organizers and designers.

My goal is that whoever you are and whatever you do, you will get helpful insights and instantly useful ideas. My hope is that you will have the courage to try some new things and have success that motivates you to try even more. My dream is that version *Two* will contain even more Best Practices from people that I don't even know yet.

When my friend Jesse read my early iterations of the book, he said, "You're not writing a book, you're creating a MOVEMENT!" And, when the movement is successful, we will all benefit.

"I listen visually."

When I am capturing information, at first, people marvel at the artistry of what I'm doing. Then, something happens: they understand that it's not really about the pretty pictures, but it's about deep listening, about truly understanding process and then synthesizing that information in a format useful to the group. Some call this design thinking. I know, based on the work of Dr. John Medina and others, most of us learn visually. That means that when I am doing my work, I am helping others to make meaning from what they are hearing and accelerate their ability to do something amazing as a result. My hope is that by creating a visual book, you will have the same accelerated learning experience, and be motivated to try new things.

"Done is better than perfect."

Sheryl Sandberg, in her book *Lean In*, said it's more important to finish something than to get it absolutely right. This is the hardest part of stopping and publishing a book. There is so much more I'd like to include, more interviews to gather information, more ideas to collect. And, if my dream comes true, this will be the first of many books.

But, for now, this is my gift to you. I hope you enjoy reading and learning from it as much as I enjoyed pulling it all together.

"Iterate, Iterate, Iterate."
Here's to you, Bill Wilmot.

Contents

To Mysti,
Who insists on mixing play with my work, and

To Kylah and Allie,
Who inspire me to do my best.

I'm happier for it.

START Meeting Model

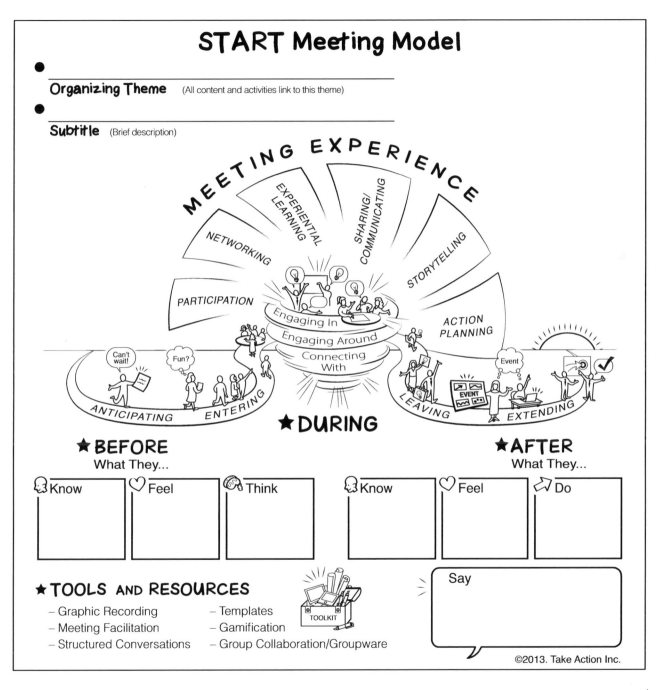

Organizing Theme (All content and activities link to this theme)

Subtitle (Brief description)

MEETING EXPERIENCE

EXPERIENTIAL LEARNING

SHARING/ COMMUNICATING

NETWORKING

STORYTELLING

PARTICIPATION

ACTION PLANNING

Engaging In
Engaging Around
Connecting With

Can't wait!

Fun?

Event

EVENT

ANTICIPATING   ENTERING

★ DURING

LEAVING   EXTENDING

★ BEFORE
What They...

★ AFTER
What They...

Know   Feel   Think

Know   Feel   Do

★ TOOLS AND RESOURCES

– Graphic Recording
– Meeting Facilitation
– Structured Conversations

– Templates
– Gamification
– Group Collaboration/Groupware

TOOLKIT

Say

©2013. Take Action Inc.

Chapter 1: Why Are We Here Anyway?

This conference was a galactic waste of my time!

It's official; this conference was a stupid idea!

Why did I even decide to come in the first place?

One summer, I decided to invest in myself. I made arrangements to go to an annual, week-long industry event: a gathering of professional speakers at the National Speakers Association (NSA) Convention. As a fledging speaker, I thought I knew what I was getting myself into. I've facilitated conferences all around the globe for almost twenty years. This was going to be a BIG conference, almost 2,000 attendees from all over the world, with some BIG personalities—speakers are not known for being reserved or quiet.

Beforehand, I talked with a few colleagues (each an experienced speaker) who were also attending, and they gave me advice:

"Focus on watching great speakers and what they do that makes them great."

"Have in mind three answers you seek."

"Don't feel like you have to attend everything; remember to take some down time to recharge your batteries."

I even decided to sign up for a full day pre-conference, the topic was one of my core passions: storytelling. I know that while conferences often cover a variety of topics, there's a lack of depth in any particular subject, and this way I would immerse myself in one subject of personal interest. So, it came as no surprise that by the time the actual conference began, I was already a bit tired.

By the end of Day One, I was exhausted—so many great ideas, so many incredible speakers in both keynote and breakout sessions to watch for both technique and message! Given my propensity for visual note taking, I was capturing beautiful, detailed notes of each speaker.

Soon, I got caught up in the fever. I was looking over the list of audiotapes available for purchase of all the breakout sessions I was unable to attend. I bought twelve of them in MP3 format so I could download them myself and listen later. Of course, you can guess, a year later I had listened to exactly ZERO of the MP3s.

I was so absorbed in the activities and my own feeling of being overwhelmed that it took me a day or two to look up and notice how many other faces were as glazed as mine surely was. Even the seasoned speakers were looking weary. By the end of the week, I was beyond tired. My feet hurt from heels that weren't made for the endless walking involved in conferences. My face

hurt from smiling at my new network of colleagues. My eyes hurt from the strain of trying to focus in darkened meeting rooms, with artificial lighting and the ever-present PowerPoint slides—most of which were poorly done and not meant for reading. The few chances I had for down time, I seized the opportunity to walk outside. Despite the Midwest summer heat, I had a strong desire to take in natural oxygen and sunlight.

In the end, despite many good sessions and a great venue, the event left me feeling weary, confused, and inadequate. I had paid out of my own pocket to come, and now I was wondering if it was worth the investment.

WHY CONFERENCES DON'T WORK

This experience was not unique, of course. As a facilitator by trade, I'm usually working during the conference, so I'm focused on the overall event and I am not there to learn or network. But, most business people can tell you their conference experiences are the same:

- Over-scheduled agendas.
- Speakers who are unprepared, unrehearsed, or are just bad speakers, all of which often lead to an over-reliance on poorly designed PowerPoint presentations. (How many times have speakers apologized for their "eye charts"?)

- A feeling of being herded from one session to the next because so much has been crammed into the conference schedule.
- Available food that is empty, carb-heavy (a.k.a., cheap), and nutrition poor, which means sugar spikes followed by the inevitable crashes.
- Not enough time to make meaningful connections or network with colleagues.
- No time to assimilate the conference learnings and determine how to apply them to real life.
- Conference theme and key messages are not conveyed or taken back home effectively, if at all.

And these are just a few of the sentiments that easily come to mind. *Sound familiar?*

What a waste of time! And how does this affect the attendees?

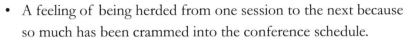

Often, people resent having to take time out of their normal responsibilities and workload to come to these events—sometimes at the request (command) of their employers. Others see these events as an escape, a chance to hang out with seldom seen colleagues. They refer to them as "boondoggles," especially if they're in desirable resort locations (funny how many meetings I facilitate in Arizona during the winter).

WHY WE GO

There are two main reasons people attend conferences:

1. To learn NEW leading-edge insights.
2. To meet NEW people.

I will be coming back to the needs of conference, event, or meeting goers over and over throughout the course of this book. I will repeat them until they are burned into your memory. The reasons people get on planes or in their cars and give their valuable time and money to come to an event may be the most important thing you can take from this book.

Your audience wants something. In order to be successful, you must give it to them, and more. It's possible, it's not painful, and it's within your control to make them happy. Why wouldn't you do it?

Lenny Lind, Founder and Chairman of CoVision, a San Francisco based company focused on turning presentations into group-wide conversations using interactive technology, explains how we ended up in all those terrible meetings: "There are many people, especially in years past, who are the designers of meetings who are basically somebody's administrative assistant. They were given the task of pulling it together and they just don't have a big enough perspective to even gauge what our value is, we become just a number." Lind has created a thriving business providing alternatives to that scenario.

Throughout the book, I will be drawing upon the experiences of my clients, as well as the expertise of my peers and mentors, like Lind, in the fields of Organizational Development, Graphic Facilitation, Presentations, and Leadership Development to show you how you can *START Meeting Like This*.

Understanding the mindset of participants and the ideas and successes of thought leaders will give you everything you need to create the meetings you dream of: engaged, participatory, successful, long-lasting, and with huge ROI.

WHAT GOES WRONG

Remember: Your attendees want to connect with new people and ideas and yet, statistically, most attendees sit next to people they already know and never re-read their notes, let alone follow up on insights they heard upon return to the office.

Here are some startling statistics:

- 91% of meeting attendees admit to daydreaming.
- 39% say they have dozed off in meetings.
- 73% say they have done other work in the midst of meetings.

So, why don't conference planners do something different?

Some have tried, like investing in electronic registration to increase efficiency, but *effectiveness* has still been overlooked. There's a built-in conflict between wanting to bring in as many attendees as possible to fill seats and pay for expensive name brand presenters and expensive venues, versus wanting to create a great conference experience for attendees.

In *Psychology Today*, writer David Rock shares the result of focusing on the first approach:

The outcome…can be measured by an informal but telling metric: the number of people in the conference sessions, versus in the hallways, on the 2nd and 3rd day of an event. (Often), the hallways were packed by the end of day two. People's brains couldn't take any more.

In an attempt to create a valuable experience for attendees, conference planners may go overboard thinking, "We have to cram the event with so much content that it appears to be worth the investment. Corporate managers sending employees to these events want to squeeze the most value out of the investment, especially if these events are a means to earn credits for professional certifications." This backfires for reasons you will understand as we go.

According to Meeting Planners International (MPI), organizers know that they should do something different and that there's nothing more important to determining the success (i.e., true value) of their meetings than defining clear objectives. And yet, when confronted, many meeting planners will claim they can't because they don't know how or it's someone else's job. Of course, nothing could be further from the truth.

MPI outlines what's referred to as The Meeting Value Chain, which goes something like this:

Needs -> Goals -> Objectives -> Activities -> Outcomes -> Impacts -> Needs

The Meeting Value Chain ensures that the needs, goals, and objectives that are established for meetings are aligned with actual outcomes and ultimately, business impact. If any of these elements are omitted or

removed, the value chain of a meeting is interrupted and there won't be a connection or translation of needs to outcomes or impacts.

However, most meeting planners will, at best, pay lip service to this approach, or at worst, ignore it completely. They're driven either by a business-as-usual mentality or by external pressure to maximize short-term gains at the expense of real results.

Here's something for you to think about as you read further:

What frustrates you personally about attending conferences/retreats/events?
When you think about just ONE THING that would make it better, what would it be?

HIGH ENGAGEMENT MEETINGS

What you are looking for in a conference has a name and some very solid theories behind it. It's called engagement and it brings you High Engagement Meetings.

The type of events, conferences, and meetings that allow you to sleep, dream, work, or otherwise check out are low on the Engagement scale and therefore low on providing attendees with the exact things they came for—meeting new people and taking in new ideas.

To turn this boring meeting into meeting bliss, leaders and conveners need to up the participation of the attendees to wake them up, keep them out of a sugar coma, and get them thinking, learning, and connecting with each other and the ideas.

A High Engagement Meeting aims to create and build interest and connection with others . . . and then, once they've got that engagement, they are able to make stuff happen. In other words, get to OUTCOMES.

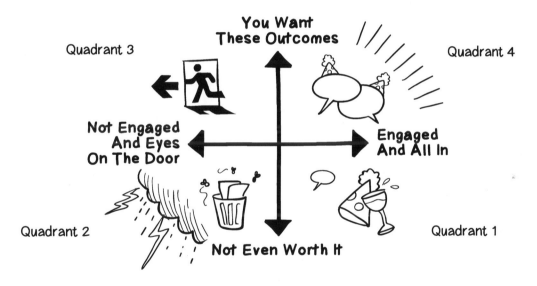

There are four ways to tell if you're creating a High Engagement Meeting. In the graph above, you're aiming for the top right of the four quadrants—high on engagement, high on outcomes.

Quadrant One: If everyone's engaged, happy, singing sweet songs, but you'll work on the outcomes next time . . . you're still not creating a truly effective meeting. You're simply hosting an expensive party.

Quadrant Two: If you're not getting the engagement and not getting the outcomes, that's a place that no one wants to be.

Quadrant Three: If you're getting great outcomes, but dragging people along, that's not exactly high engagement.

Quadrant Four: This is the sweet spot. You have created engagement and productive outcomes.

Show the participants at your next workshop the model. Get them to tell you how well you did with engagement *and* outcomes. Feedback is essential to planning a great event and knowing how you did lets you do even better the next time.

You may well be somewhere between these, but whatever you do, keep striving to create engagement *and* productive results. The people you work with are counting on you.

SUMMARY

Meetings can be overwhelming and exhausting if they are poorly planned. They can be exciting and captivating if you do it right. Keep in mind the things that make meetings awful and strive to avoid them. Keep in mind where you want to be on the graph (hint: High Outcomes/High Engagement) and what kind of leader or planner you want to be (hint: not boring or simply a party planner). If you can take the time to set goals and objectives and make sure the needs of your attendees are taken care of, you will have successful meetings.

Chapter 2: And Yet, We Still Have Conferences

I knew the event was going to be huge.

My client had asked me to graphically record at a conference for 9,000 people to be held in multiple Disney World venues. Normally, I would've gotten there a day ahead to get the lay of the land and know my way around. Instead, I arrived the evening before, as the attendees did, so I experienced what they may have been experiencing: pure pandemonium.

The first day of the conference was overwhelming from the moment I got to the central pavilion to register. So many people wandering around in every direction, packed agendas, and multiple keynotes and workshops across a variety of co-located hotels. Now, I'm a seasoned conference attendee as my work takes me to events of all shapes and sizes around the globe. I've worked on both internal events and industry-specific conferences as small as 60 people to as large as 9,000 people. While I was at this event, I polled several people at the first evening dinner and each response validated mine: "I'm totally overwhelmed."

WE ARE SOCIAL ANIMALS

If we know quantity doesn't equal quality, then why do we still meet this way? We have more technology available than ever before, more ways to videoconference, and yet the conference business is BOOMING. *Why is this?* Speaker and author of *Start With Why*, Simon Sinek, asserts that humans have a basic need to connect. Even bloggers, whose sole purpose is to write for a virtual audience, meet face to face at an annual conference in Las Vegas.

Meetup.com, which facilitates offline group meetings held all over the world on every topic imaginable, began in New York City after 9/11. The two New York-based founders were influenced by two things:

1. *Bowling Alone*, Robert Putnam's book about the collapse of community in America, and
2. After September 11th, they noticed that something had changed in New York: strangers had started saying hello and people seemed suddenly aware of each other. There was a yearning for community.

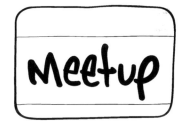

The founders wanted to use the Internet as a way to connect people of like interests, and Meetup.com became an easy way to do this. I often sit in a Meetup—a live meeting held at a coffee shop, library, or other public place—of strangers who share one common goal: to write a book. There are Meetups on every business or personal interest topic you can imagine, from marketing and networking to hiking and raw food. These are loose events without all the rigmarole that goes with a conference, but they demonstrate people's inherent need to get together and talk about things in which they have an interest.

On any given day, thousands of conferences, events, or retreats are being held across the globe. So, it doesn't look like conferences are going away! The actual hotels where these events are held change based on what's popular or new, often booked a year or more in advance. Speakers are booked based on what topics are hot and in the news. And the swag bags—gift packages handed out to every attendee—are filled with whatever fits the conference theme or is trending that month. But, the show must go on, and the speakers must get their keynotes, and the attendees must get their fixes of new (really?) content—much to the delight of all the meeting and event planners who are employed to make these events successful.

WE ARE NOT GETTING THE MOST OUT OF MEETING

But are these events really meeting their goals? Attendees I've asked suggest some very basic goals:

- To learn something new.
- To meet colleagues who can provide new information or contacts.
- For some, to be a resource or seen as a "subject matter expert."

Research would show that the Millennials, or digital natives as they are called, are expecting something more than a sage on the stage. They want to not only learn something, but to be entertained in the process, something termed *edutainment*. They want to be entertained and educated at once—no boredom while being educated and no cotton candy events while being entertained.

Heck, is that desire unique to someone born between 1970 and 2000? ALL of us, if we've paid our conference fee, booked our room, traveled to a unique location, and put on our business casual attire, want to get something out of the experience. We don't want it to be boring, either! We're overwhelmed by the day-to-day information overload and the amount of tasks on our plates. We want relevant, useful information that will help us do something better, know something we didn't know, understand something better, and ultimately to make our lives somehow improved.

But we've shown up in person, darn it. We're media savvy. We want concepts (especially potentially dull ones) brought to life, and we expect to be entertained, perhaps even involved, while we have these experiences. We want to connect to ideas.

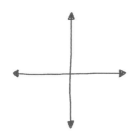

"We live in times of high stress. Messages that are simple, messages that are inspiring, messages that are life-affirming, are a welcome break from our real lives."

— Simon Sinek, Author of *Start With Why*

One of the best ways to tell that a meeting is in the snooze zone is when the need to connect is happening through technology, mostly with people not in the room. If people pull out their phones and start texting, WORRY. Unless you have made technology part of your event, which is in Chapter 12, then you should NOT be proud.

There are so many ways people connect with others, from Facebook posts to website blogs to Twitter tweets. People are longing for some way to connect with others, even beyond who they're sharing a meeting room with, to validate their experience and share their learnings with a wider audience.

I've had conversations with colleagues talking about the behavior of people in meetings where distractions abound. The best thing about changing from a Blackberry to an cell phone was losing that blinking red light that told me someone had contacted me (and didn't I need to respond… RIGHT NOW? It was clearly urgent; the blinking red light was like a siren).

Iris Firstenberg, Adjunct Associate Professor of UCLA, shares research that indicates dopamine is released when we are resolving crises, which include the immediacy of responding to emails and texts. So, when planning a meeting, you are up against the mobile phone addiction and you need to be at least that captivating and engaging to get them to fight the need to get a dopamine hit.

As I walk into a room to facilitate a session, I'm shocked at how commonplace it is for people to have their laptops or smart phones on, responding to emails as the group works on developing business strategies. How can they focus on the big picture of developing the future of their business while they're replying to an email from a colleague about a business lunch a week away?

Newsflash: WE DON'T MULTI-TASK WELL

The answer is simple: *they can't*. While people WANT to believe, DESPERATELY want to believe, that they're good at multi-tasking, research has proven this is just not the case. Social critic Linda Stone has coined the term "continuous partial attention" to describe the fractured way we now focus. "With continuous partial attention," Stone explains, "we keep the top level item in focus and scan the periphery in case something more important emerges."

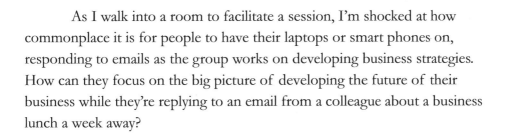

Or something more alluring, reassuring, or simply less demanding. A recent *Harvard Business Review* post says that multi-tasking leads to as much as a 40% drop in productivity, increased stress, and a 10% drop in IQ! For those who still argue that they're great at multi-tasking, research indicates that our brain is actually switching rapidly from one task to another. The take away? Do fewer things better.

Given that conferences and events are not going away, and the fact that we're using a very old model of how we organize them, what should we keep in mind from all of this data? Here are the main points:

- Events—meetings that take place face to face—serve an important purpose in terms of helping people feel connected.

- Creating community is a critical element to design into successful events.

- Figuring out how to incorporate productive outlets for social media during an event is critical.

- People can't effectively multi-task, so they need to be engaged in a single task that serves their needs so the distractions will be put away by choice.

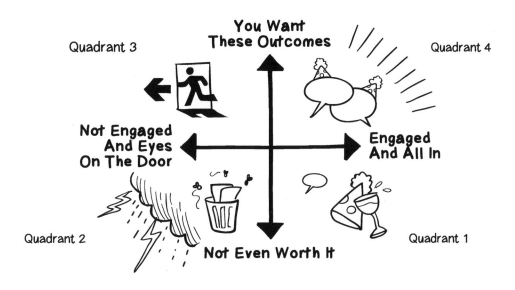

Knowing all that we know now, it's possible to create meetings that fly right out of the Snooze Zone and into High Engagement/Productivity.

SUMMARY

Our need to learn and connect with each other is not going to go away. We are, by nature, social and storytelling animals who want to connect with each other and with ideas. We need to create meetings and events where people are so actively engaged that they put away their distractions by choice, which is good, because people can't really multi-task anyway.

Chapter 3: Then Let's Do It Differently!

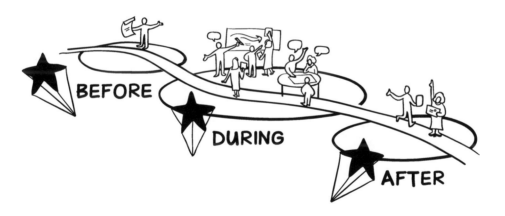

The Cavallo Point Conference Center, at the foot of the Golden Gate Bridge, was a spectacular location for a week-long summit.

The event had been carefully thought out from beginning to end. Food was selected and prepared with health and nutrition in mind. Thought was also put into giving people a chance to experience wellness through things like guided yoga sessions.

Brian Camastral, CEO of Riversong Sanctuary, Cofounder of BLITS Foundation, and former Global President of a large CPG company, and one of the organizers of the conference, started out with a huge goal: He set out to shift the mindset of his entire organization.

The first thing you shift is mindset, then you shift behaviors, and finally you shift results. Most people focus on the results. They might get better short term results, but not good long term results. However, when you shift the mindset first, you get different behaviors followed by better, sustainable results.

Camastral explained, "The purpose of the summit was to shift the mindset so that people could imagine what was possible and to unleash their imaginations and energy, so they would run off in that direction."

To achieve his goal, Camastral needed a powerful event, and he and his team created one.

WHAT MAKES A POWERFUL EVENT

A powerful event has three parts: a BEFORE, a DURING, and an AFTER. It sounds basic, after all, plays and movies and even books are written this way—with three parts: a beginning, a middle, and an end. What happens in creating a successful meeting using the START Meeting Model is anything but basic. You get engagement, action, collaboration, excitement, output, retention, and ROI.

Each part of the START Meeting Model is made up of the design elements you need to consider to make your meeting a raving success.

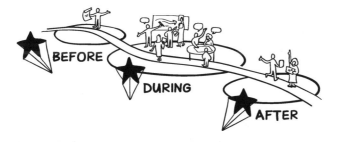

The rest of this book will explore the START Meeting Model and travel through brain science, Organization Development, expert interviews,

and theories to explain why this works and why you should use it. You will get to hear voices from all over the business world that corroborate and build on the START Meeting Model.

I will not leave you hanging. Each section of the START Meeting Model will come with a Best Practices chapter to show you how to implement the ideas. These are practices drawn from the real life experience of leaders in the field. You can use any of them—the tricks and tips— tomorrow and your meetings will take off. This practical guide gives you ways to put your new knowledge to work for you right away.

DESIGNING SUCCESS

To start planning any truly stellar event, conference, or meeting, use what author Steven Covey would refer to as "Habit Two: Begin with the end in mind." Covey said, "One has to know where they are going to make sure that they are headed in the right direction." Conference organizers and organization leaders who are clear on what they want attendees to get out of the conference from the get-go will always have better results.

"If you don't know where you're going, you'll end up somewhere else."

— Yogi Berra, American former Major League Baseball player

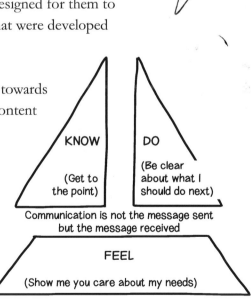

Agenda design is the way to be conscious of your event and meeting the needs of your participants. Take, for example, the meeting that opened this chapter. The agenda was designed so it was purposely not over-scheduled; there were deliberate breaks in the program intended for content digestion during down time and relaxation. Many call this "creating space." Camastral was very conscientious about protecting thinking and reflection time for his team. Unlike so many other leaders, he wouldn't think of scheduling "working lunches."

Together, the organizers created a core theme for the conference, and then incorporated powerful speakers, visual elements, and breakouts that allowed people to integrate what they had learned. I was there working as one of three graphic facilitators, and the graphic wall charts we created were distributed to each attendee in a format designed for them to remember the content and move forward on actions that were developed over the course of the week.

Everything about the conference was designed towards the participants taking in and integrating the meeting content and then holding on to it once they left.

Communication experts refer to this as the bottom line of communication:

KNOW
(Get to the point)

DO
(Be clear about what I should do next)

Communication is not the message sent but the message received

FEEL
(Show me you care about my needs)

1. What do we want participants to KNOW? (Convey information)
2. How do we want them to FEEL? (Or believe)
3. As a result, what do we want them to DO? (Take action)

And I would add one more: what do we want people to be SAYING as a result of this experience? What are the stories they will remember and share with others?

These four goals often intersect, of course—the process of getting someone to take some action may sometimes involve conveying information along with persuasion. The way to think about conferences, therefore, is to start with the goal and work backward to the design.

With that in mind, here's the key question: *What is the purpose of the gathering?*

Given the potential, conferences have to make a lasting impact on the attendees. It seems fitting to look at the amazing possibilities there are for these events to reinvent themselves. We need to put the focus on the EXPERIENCE—with the goal of creating events that are more useful, more productive, more effective, and . . . (gasp!) more FUN! Focusing on these two key areas seems like a good way to begin:

1. How is the conference itself designed?
2. How can opportunities for networking and interaction be created?

THE DESIGN OF THE CONFERENCE EXPERIENCE

Greg Bogue, Experience Architect for Maritz Travel, works to help his clients design an experience for their events. He creates a mindset about conference design, "I think when people talk in terms of attendee or guest experience they think in terms of engagement. How do we engage the people more effectively? How can we create a community? That's a huge one. If we can get event designers thinking of themselves as community builders, that would be a powerful thing. Focus on community."

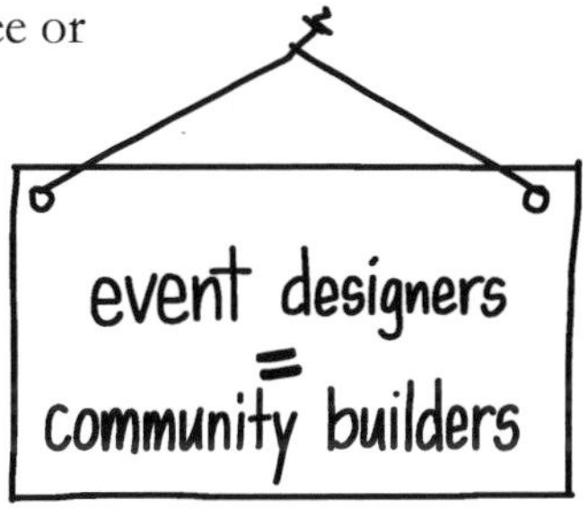

A well-designed, engaging conference should be as commonplace in business as cell phones are to daily life. Remember the days before mobile phones? Some day, you will be remembering back to the days before transformative, engaging meetings.

In 2005, according to biographer Walter Isaacson, CEO Steve Jobs worried that Apple was missing a key market: cell phones. As he looked at all the phones on the market, he noticed something: cell phones were ALL bad. Does that sound familiar? Like meetings, while everyone had a cell phone,

event designers = community builders

everyone was very unhappy with their phone experience.

At the time, Jobs and his team were working on the infancy stages of the iPad. As they sat around brainstorming, they talked about how much they hated their phones—they were too complicated and had features no one could figure out, including the address book. Apple put the iPad on the back burner and instead began a quest to build a phone that THEY would want to use. As Plato said, "Necessity is the mother of invention."

Jobs' strongly held belief was that people didn't even know what they wanted until they were shown. We accept bad phones and bad conferences because bad is the only way we have known it. I can tell you from experience though, once you have gone to an engaging conference or meeting where you achieve all of your goals and feel connected, being at a Snooze Fest is like going back to texting on one of those old fashioned phones where you had to scroll through the numbers and letters each time you typed a text message.

Once the iPhone was built and people began using it, it was unimaginable to return to the past. Now imagine having the same disruptive impact on the conference experience. Imagine designing a conference experience that, say five years from now, people couldn't imagine NOT having! Tools such as the PowerPoint "eye charts" that today

are created and passed off as effective presentations—so commonplace, in fact, they are today considered normal—would enrage people so much that they would walk out of a room. It would be like someone handing you a flip phone to use today.

Stay with me. We are talking about building a community of engaged participants with great outcomes and huge ROI.

This is what the iPhone of meetings would look like using the START Meeting Model:

Before the event, imagine being contacted via a video from the organizers—maybe showing what the venue looked like, perhaps even a visual overview of what the sessions would cover, and something about the key themes of the conference. Maybe you would even get something fun in the mail ahead of time related to the theme—teasers that had you intrigued and excited about your upcoming experience.

Once on-site, you'd feel like an effort had been made to really make you feel a part of the event, not just a passive participant. There would be fun, playful, wall-sized boards that invited your participation. The theme of the

conference would be interwoven into various parts of the experience. Visual murals would be created of the plenary sessions (both in hard copy and electronically using an iPad), which were then posted in a common space,

with opportunities to comment on the speaker's message, as well as get paper copies of the charts to remember what you'd heard. All the charts would be available electronically; you'd use the QR code posted nearby to download them onto your device.

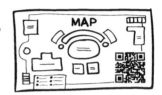

Throughout the conference, you'd be encouraged to tweet insights, with #hashtags, which were collated so you could see what others were saying. There would be a common website set up to post photos from the event, so everyone from the meeting could see not only the pictures they took, but those taken by fellow attendees. A conference website would curate related conference materials and conversations so you could virtually connect with others. There would be time built into the conference for participants to make their own personal connections between new insights and practical application.

There would be just the right amount of information presented in sessions tailored to get you out of multi-task mode and into the material. You have space between sessions to meet your fellow conference goers and trade insights and to integrate what you learned. You would have notes, video, graphic maps, and other multi-media take always from your participation.

Once you were back in your office, the event would still be available to you. A summary graphic would have been created and animated with an audio track that summarized the themes of the conference so you could share with your team and colleagues. In it, there would be embedded videos, photos, and graphics that took you back to the event like it had happened yesterday.

All this is possible!

BRAIN SCIENCE BACKS US UP

I've seen all of these elements, and more, done at conferences around the world, using powerful visual techniques like whiteboard animation, tablet scribing, graphic facilitation, graphic recording, and sketch noting. These ideas are catching on like wildfire. Take a look at some of the newest, hottest books: *Back of the Napkin*, *Visual Meetings*, and *Business Model Generation*. Since Daniel Pink used whiteboard animation to describe his *Drive* theories around human behavior, the technique has been used over and over in just about every situation, from explaining to teaching to selling.

Dr. John Medina, author of *Brain Rules*, shares useful rules of how the brain works. Here are a few that relate to the conference world:

Rule #4: We don't pay attention to boring things. Humans can only pay attention for short bursts, and then energy drops. Dr. Medina suggests changing gears every ten minutes in your presentation. Tell a relevant story, show a relevant video, play relevant music, do a relevant activity, etc.

Rule #5: Repeat to remember. Our brain learns through repetition in timed intervals. This means the central theme needs to be repeated on a regular basis to make it memorable. You can improve your chances of remembering something if you reproduce the environment in which you first put it in your brain. Remember this as you think about the value of creating visuals.

Rule #10: Vision is our dominant sense—it trumps ALL OTHER SENSES. We have better recall for visual information and we're incredible at remembering pictures. That's why visual methodologies work so well. Medina says if you hear a piece of information, you're likely to remember 10% of it three days later. Add a picture and you'll remember 65%.

"Pictures beat text . . . because reading is so inefficient for us. We have to identify certain features in the letters to be able to read them. That takes time."

— Dr. John Medina, Author of *Brain Rules*

AN OUTLINE FOR PLANNING

Janine Underhill, Founder and CEO of Idea 360 – The Art of Possibility and Amplify the Impact, uses a clearly defined process when she is working with clients to plan a meeting or conference. She meets with her clients several times before the meeting, "the earlier the better," she says, to plan every aspect of the goals and messages so that when participants arrive, live the meeting, and go home, they learn and remember the key points. Here is her plan:

Ask yourself the following questions:

In the design phase . . .

- WHAT do we want this meeting to do for us over the long term?
- WHAT do we want people to be doing differently in two or three months?
- WHAT do we want them to know or learn to guide actions or behavior?
- WHAT key ideas do we want to leverage for the time period we are focusing on?
- WHO is in the audience and HOW do they best receive information?
- WHO are my storytellers?

 In the actual meeting . . .

- WHAT are we capturing to use later?
- Start to reinforce the big messages NOW and think about the RULE of SEVEN (see Best Practices for After the Meeting)!
- At the beginning: tell them what you are going to tell them! At the end: tell them what you told them!
- Remember: what is not captured during the meeting CAN NOT be replicated!
- The Rule of Seven—you need to present information seven times in different formats to ensure people get it.

 After the meeting . . .

- Start to make the artifacts developed during the meeting available QUICKLY—we mean as soon as the next morning
- Borrowing from education—tell them again what you told them
- Provide information in forms that meet the participants learning styles—visual, auditory, high level or in detail.
- Use the information immediately—show action!

"Knowing is not enough; we must apply.
Willing is not enough; we must DO."

— Johann Wolfgang von Goethe, Poet/Philosopher

AFTER THE AFTER - AMPLIFY THE IMPACT!

- MOST IMPORTANTLY—invigorate a team of storytellers to carry the message. Most often, this means hosting a workshop to remind your folks how to tell a story. If you can schedule this before the meeting, they will be working on your behalf.
- Task these storytellers with helping to put the information into forms that they think will be most effective to reach the audience.
- Craft a set of speaking points in a simple format that allows people to add what is most important to them while reinforcing the messages.
- Really understand WHAT is in it for the audience—WHY is this information important and what kinds of issues is it working to solve?
- Use the captured content from the meeting to help you springboard your messages. Think about your demographic and curate the content appropriately.

OPPORTUNITIES FOR NETWORKING AND INTERACTION

Now that we have thought about our goals, we can think about the actual user experience. Remember, users want to interact with each other and with new ideas and our job is to facilitate their needs. Currently, people tend to feel herded and alienated at events. Conversely, if it's a corporate conference, people sit with people who are safe, known, and comfortable. How can we maximize the networking possibilities if this is the case?

I work with a team at Stanford Research Institute (SRI) who run sessions in which international groups come to Silicon Valley to learn about innovation, partly by visiting start-ups and learning how they work. Two presenters, both experienced investors, shared how the concept of networking operates within the valley. Some of the tips included:

- Hold events that are learning events, held for the events' sake, not for selling.
- *Gamification* is the purposeful design of experiences so they feel game-like, engage people often through technology, and take advantage of humans' desire to play.
- Draw in people from varied skill sets and backgrounds with great speakers, short events, and gamification techniques to make them fun.
- Share both event schedules and content freely to create a buzz.

At a conference where I was working, the concept of gamification was discussed in terms of how to apply to learning. Gamification is the process of using game thinking and game mechanics to engage audiences, and it creates an environment where everyone can have a unique experience within the event.

Using the original Bartle Test of Gamer Psychology (yes, there is such a thing), gamers are categorized into one of four categories: 10% of the population are Explorers, 1% are Killers (I think I'm glad this number is low), 9% are Achievers, and 80% are Socializers. Focus for a minute on that last number: this means *four out of five people want to take part in activities that allow them to be interactive players.*

Now, combine this with the concepts put forward in *Driven: How Human Nature Shapes Our Choices* by authors Paul Lawrence and Nitin Nohria. Lawrence and Nohria's four drive theory helps to explain what humans want, as well as *why* they want those things. On the whole, humans love to:

- **Acquire**—both material goods, as well as immaterial things like status, power, and influence.
- **Bond**—form relationships and interact with other people.
- **Learn**—explore new areas of life, practice new skills, and satisfy curiosity.
- **Defend**—protect what is "ours," and drive away threats to our safety and security.

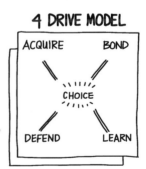

How does this play out from a gamification standpoint?

When gamification is done well, it addresses all of these needs so everyone is able to participate in a manner that takes into account their own personal preferences.

"The four drives are universal," cites Josh Kaufman. "They transcend age, status, and culture. The drives describe the human experience, and we all want all of them all of the time. As a result, these drives are useful when examining how people are currently behaving, as well as predicting how they're likely to behave in the future."

Just to drive the point home, take a look at the sample scenario of engaging attendees through thoughtful incorporation of gamification principles, provided from Rajat Paharia's book *Loyalty 3.0: How to Revolutionize Customer and Employee Engagement with Big Data and Gamification*. Paharia's key design drivers are:

- PERSONAL—"A one-size-fits-all approach will feel shallow and will risk confusing and alienating participants."

- COLLABORATIVE—"An experience focused solely on individuals won't work. [...] It becomes hard to connect in any meaningful way with other people and is easy to just be a faceless part of the crowd."

- REWARDING—"Prosocial incentives (rewards that you give to other people rather than keep for yourself) have been shown to increase performance more than standard incentives do. The key is to use a mix of both."

Like gamification, we know a great deal about how networking and interaction work from the experience of co-working and the theories and practices that have come out of it. Co-working is when you bring people together from various locations, backgrounds, and experiences to work together, expanding the possibilities for creativity and innovation.

> **"Conversations, as you already know, are the core of relationships. And relationships are the core of business, because we all want to do business with people we like."**

— Jezra Kaye, Speaker Coach, Speak Up for Success

In the design of conferences today, these networking opportunities are mostly lost because the majority of people don't know how to network effectively and aren't given the time and space to do it anyway, let alone share their knowledge and experience. If you create a space for people to have less formal interactions than designed presentations, they will have the potential

to really share ideas as well as create relationships. Two for the price of one! The concept is proven in the start-up world, but it is just moving into the conference world.

"Many people profess the best experiences they have when attending conferences, trade shows, conventions and other business gatherings come from the people they meet. The hallway conversations after a keynote or a concurrent session are often where people process the information and share real life information with their peers. The act of discussing the experience of the presentation and curriculum allow the shared knowledge to be digested and expanded. This 'hallway networking' is an important part of the learning."

—Thom Singer, Author

"Think about all of the greatest moments in your life for a second - the experiences that shaped you, the conversations you had, the milestones. They all probably share one thing in common: they were with the people who mean the most to you. Heck, they were with people in general. The same goes for work. Being in a place where you can talk to people, bounce ideas off others, and feel connected to the world outside your house helps make your work more vital. You might even make a friend or two."

— Mitch Holt, Author

Tony Hsieh knows about the importance of interaction in expanding one's thinking. Hsieh is the CEO of Zappos, and he remembers when many start-ups, before and up to Zappos, in San Francisco, were fueled by people co-working and sparking creativity through accidental conversations. Fast forward to Las Vegas, where Zappos' headquarters is located. Hsieh has taken on a new project he calls "The Downtown Project." His dream? To create the co-working capital of the world—the idea that common spaces need to be created so people from different disciplines bump into each other, whether it be over a beer, in a yoga class, or walking their dogs. These bumps spark conversation, and the conversation leads to ideas, innovation, engagement, and better work.

Steve Jobs actually designed this co-working concept into the architectural space of Pixar Studios. For our purposes, co-learning is a take off on the co-working concept. In other words, the same thing can happen at conferences and events. Maximize interaction and you maximize engagement.

To facilitate co-learning in your conferences and meetings you can take some simple steps:

- Create space for conversations to occur by not over-scheduling the agenda and allowing downtime.
- Design time for structured conversations to happen spontaneously, via posted questions or polling that allows for interaction.
- Consider gamification techniques, such as creating teams within a large group, so people have a chance to meet people they would not have ordinarily met.

Summary

Begin with the end in mind. Start slow to go gangbusters. Spend time designing your events and conferences around the outcomes you want: the feelings, ideas, and connections you want your attendees to take with them. Make sure every conference incorporates key ingredients necessary for a successful meeting experience: Participation, Networking, Experiential Learning, Sharing and Communication, Storytelling, and Action Planning.

Use brain science to make sure you optimize participation and fun. This means make it visual, make it interactive, and make it a game and/or a learning opportunity.

Chapter 4: Before They Get There

At the end of a three-day offsite for a global company, a group of its senior executives took the last half of the day to outline what they wanted to accomplish during their upcoming conference with their Global Top 120. A gathering like this hadn't happened in nearly twenty years, and yet, the business desperately needed reassurance from leadership about the direction they should take.

I stood in front of a large piece of paper and sketched out the ideas as they came tumbling out of people's mouths. The group decided their three main objectives for the conference:

1. To present a new vision and clarify key roles for the company.
2. To share and get input on the five core business strategies.
3. To create actions to move the needle for the organization toward the vision and implement creative ways to engage others.

With this skeleton laid out, it was easy to craft an agenda that would achieve these objectives, although great thought would be put into the how. The next step: to figure out how to arrange all the logistics in just six weeks! But the work they put into thinking about the agenda would set them up for success in planning.

IT'S ALL ABOUT THE PLANNING

Let's bring back the START Meeting Model:

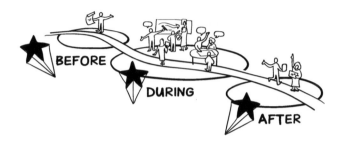

Logistically, quite a bit of preparation goes into planning a large conference or meeting or event. Finding a site big enough to hold the number of people expected, along with meeting rooms, sleeping rooms, and food for meals and breaks—are all essential components of any conference. Transportation is often coordinated, and offsite activities are sometimes part of the planning.

Then there's the design of the event itself: hopefully someone has put more thought into it than, "We always meet in February." Objectives for why people would want to attend must be created first, and from there would be deciding what keynotes, breakouts, and workshops should occur to support those objectives. This is sometimes even more critical when the attendee has

made the choice to attend and is paying out of their own pocket but, the fact remains—the event needs to be well-designed.

Using the START Meeting Model, you will address every aspect of the experience and the message and make sure your participants leave with what they came looking for and what you needed them to internalize. It's a win-win if you design with the START Meeting Model.

Hayler Foster, a Short Talk Expert, professional speaker, and the author of *Don't Tank Your TED Talk*, talks about the meeting design in this way:

> There is something which I term "the full ride experience." Let's take a one-day event that's going from 8:30 am to 6:00 pm. From the moment that the participants step onto the venue property to the time they leave, we orchestrate the totality of their experience.
>
> Always have a theme for a conference. In a theme, you want to be broad enough that you can do many diverse things, but specific enough that it makes the whole conference hang together. It's not just the content of the talks and the quality of the talks, but the order you put them in. Since the order of the talks can make or break a program, it is important for somebody who has an intimate knowledge of every single speaker's content to arrange them. For example, typically, I'll open with someone highly energetic. I will

put a presenter before lunch who is impactful enough that people are talking about the presentation over lunch. Every minute is intentional; it's intentional to create a serendipitous experience.

Beyond the presenters, don't forget you need to plan in all of the time for networking, the gamification, the visual and the technological pieces, and make it all serve your goals for what people take home with them in how they feel, the new ideas they have, and the connections they made.

Once a "skeleton" of the overall event is designed, additional planning needs to be put into what belongs where so there's a logical flow. Appropriate speakers, whether they're members of the group or thought-provoking outside speakers, must be identified, scheduled, and budgeted. And perhaps even a conference tagline and a logo.

Those are the obvious items to decide, obvious yet very important. Your conference depends on having a goal and objectives. But what about the not-so-obvious?

✔ How do you create excitement, intrigue, and engagement before the conference even begins?

✔ Once people register for the event, how do you give them confidence in their decision to attend?

✓ How do you create enough grassroots buzz so that more people will commit to the event?

Anticipation really begins the minute someone decides, or is told, they will attend an event. Normally, anticipation consists only of figuring out airfare and how close the hotel is to the venue (sometimes the hotel IS the venue). *This is the most common lost opportunity in creating engagement and excitement for what's coming.* There are so many things that can be done to get people into the frame of mind for what is to come, from video links to articles to gamification strategies, and for connecting participants ahead of time.

> "A conversation is a dialogue, not a monologue. That's why there are so few good conversations: due to scarcity, two intelligent talkers seldom meet."

— Truman Capote, Author

The shift from Anticipating to Entering happens the moment a participant steps on site at the event location. Their experience of the actual event begins here. This can be as simple as a welcome table with nametags and packets to something much more elaborate. At one event, for example, participants were greeted with small glasses of juice and then driven to the welcome desk. In front of the desk were several tables with snacks ranging

from healthy to indulgent, as well as cool drinks ranging from fruit-infused water to margaritas. The experience immediately set a welcoming tone.

Let's take a look at each of these elements of creating a stellar conference.

BEFORE THE EVENT – ANTICIPATING & ENTERING

Stephen Zaruba and John Quereto are Partners and Regional Practice Directors for Expressworks, an organizational change consulting firm based in San Francisco Bay Area and Houston, Texas. They give the following advice in thinking about the BEFORE:

- Preparing people for the event is more important than the event.

- Invest time up front talking to each person invited and, from those conversations, you can create an operational vision for a group to impact the meeting.

- Talk with participants, individually, and say, "This is what we are trying to achieve. What do you think about that? Here is how we think we're going to run it. What do you think about that?"

- Another way is to ask people: "When are you arriving?" "Do you need help with transportation?" "Here is the hotel we've got for you. What do you like in a hotel?" It is really being respectful to have people's input solicited. A lot of them don't travel that far very often, so we try to be very sensitive to making sure that the experience is smooth and planned.

And, by the time everybody gets there, it is an amazing week. People are ready and eager to make a difference.

Management Consultant, Peter Block outlines six conversations that create accountability and commitment. His first conversation is "The Invitation Conversation."

In the Invitation Conversation, the leadership task is to name the debate, issue the invitation, and invest in those who choose to show up. Those who accept the call will bring the next circle of people into the conversation.

By naming the event (debate, as he terms it), people know what they are signing up for. Inviting people to participate allows them to choose whether they want to be part of the conversation and by showing up, they are expected to bring their best thinking and ideas.

Getting people thinking about the event and looking forward to the experience is equally as important as many of the logistical details, and yet it's so rarely done. Remember the two main goals people have for attending:

1. Learn about new, relevant information.
2. Meet and network with others with a common interest.

Hopefully attendees know ahead of time what sessions are being offered and what the overall agenda flow is. But, what can you do to really ENGAGE them in the content before they even pack their suitcases?

Recently, I attended the fourth annual *Wisdom 2.0 Conference*, held in San Francisco. I had signed up in June for the following February event. I received an immediate confirmation and then, in November, I got an email about hotel deals and how to host a breakout. That meant I could be involved in being part of the event! In December, I received an update telling me how many people were signed up and information about how to host a session via contest selection—again inviting my involvement and using a playful format. In January, a month before the event, I started getting emails telling me about some of the exciting speakers who were set to appear, big names like Ariana Huffington, of the *Huffington Post*, and Jeff Weiner, LinkedIn CEO. I found myself becoming excited about attending.

Your event may not be as big or have the same opportunities, but your goal is the same—bring people into the conference before they ever set foot in the conference space.

Luckily, there are a lot of amazing techniques to generate excitement and engagement, especially with the use of technology and creativity.

Here are just a few ideas to engage and excite people:

- Ask attendees to submit a question they would like answered during the event.
- Create an animated video that narrates highlights of the upcoming event and post it online.
- Put together a multimedia presentation that includes narration, a graphic, and short videos of conference speakers as a teaser.
- Incorporate gamification techniques to connect participants to the content and each other before they arrive.
- Create social media conversations using #hashtags.

All of these ideas become easy to incorporate when you think of them through the lens of your goals and objectives. If you want people

to leave with a strong network (their goal too), use the time before the conference to introduce people, create peer groups, give people a chance to read about each other or reach out to each other. If you want to have people leave with more knowledge of a topic or field, invite them to the conversation in advance—create a hashtag, start a blog, have them contribute resources or compete in trivia contests about the topic.

SUMMARY

Meeting design is crucial to achieving your goals and having happy participants. Once you have designed, you need a strong BEFORE to pull people in. The two parts of the START Meeting Model that deal with BEFORE are Anticipating and Entering. Making sure you address both of these is crucial. The possibilities are endless for how to successfully invite attendees. One you have set your goals and objectives, and with the most common goals of participants in mind (networking and learning) plan out ways to involve, excite, gamify, engage, and introduce your event or conference to build excitement and begin engagement well before the meeting takes place.

Chapter 5: Before - Best Practices

In this section of Best Practices, you will find hands-on ways to incorporate the START Meeting Model into any meeting, event, or conference you are planning. You can pick and choose among the ideas for whatever phase of the START Meeting Model you want to strengthen your meetings. You can combine them, adapt them to your circumstances, expand them, or make up your own. If you find something that works especially well, make sure to email us and let us know what you did and how it worked. Creating inspiring events is a creative and evolving process, and you are cordially invited to share it with us.

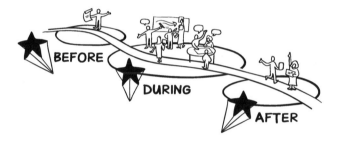

ANTICIPATING

Send Postcards to Your Participants

Email is so prevalent and mail with a stamp is so rare these days that sending mail, real old-fashioned snail mail, can be an attention grabber. Putting the conference logo, maybe a few bullets of what you'll learn, featured speakers or information about the venue can get invitees into the conference mode much better than email which can end up in the junk mail or the thousands of unread emails deemed not pressing to look at.

— Greg Bogue, Maritz Travel

Hand-Written Welcome Notes

Using the old-fashioned envelope and stamp method, one client direct mailed a note, personally signed by him, to participants welcoming them and letting them know how excited he was that they were coming and that he was looking forward to their participation. This note was sent four to six weeks prior to the event.

— Emily Shepard, The Graphic Distillery

Visual-Based PowerPoint Deck

Although PowerPoint is a very overused, misused tool, it can be effective in conveying a message out to a large audience. By using mostly images and carefully crafted text written to invite and intrigue, you can send out a PowerPoint deck as a way to give information about the event, ask thought-provoking questions and generate excitement about what is to come. It's a bit like a visual invitation. It can also be set to music so it plays like a mini-movie for the viewer.

— Brian Camastral, CEO Riversong Sanctuary, Cofounder BLITS Foundation, and former Global President of a large CPG company

Email Attachments

Sending articles relevant to the topic featured at the conference helps attendees get focused on what they'll be learning and get them in the mood for the topic. These can be either sent as a collection or sent one by one, over time.

— Dana Wright, Take Action Inc.

Email Announcements

As events are scheduled, speakers confirmed, or activities require participation, they are emailed to registered participants (and maybe even past participants as a way to entice them to register). As the event date approaches, emails become more frequent to get participants excited about the event.

— *Wisdom 2.0*, San Francisco

Leadership Story Posters

At one event, leaders were interviewed about their leadership perspective in advance of the event by a graphic recorder who drew the story digitally (using an iPad). Iterations were sent to the storyteller for review and refinement. The final posters were created and printed on a poster board so they could be used to tell their story to one another.

— Nevada Lane, Lane Change Consulting

Video Introductions

Everyone who was attending a corporate event was asked to create and upload a video to the company's YouTube account. Some people used the opportunity to spread the word about a cause they cared deeply about. Some did a quick iPhone video while on-site and just talked to the camera. Others took the camera around their house and introduced their family (one even video taped during their family's crawfish boil!). A lot of people got very creative and did mock music videos (a hilarious video done to the tune of Billy Joel's "We Didn't Start the Fire") and mock commercials (great

spoof of the Dos Equis "the most interesting man in the world"). The videos were sprinkled throughout the event—usually before or after breaks as people filtered back in. It was nice to be able to see videos of people who couldn't make it to the meeting and vice versa. The best part was laughing, and sometimes crying, during the videos. There were definitely some personal and touching moments.
— John Quereto and Vivian Li, Expressworks

Pre-Event Interviews

Conducting one-on-one interviews before events helps bring people into the process and helps them feel invited and included. By asking carefully selected questions, you can create a large visual to show the collective data.
— Sita Magnuson, depict llc.

Conference-Related Questionnaires via Email

Prior to the conference, distribute questions or surveys using tools such as Survey Monkey to get an idea of what people want to know at the event, what they already know coming in, or getting other information, all of which helps to create engagement before an event begins and helps you plan with their goals in mind.

— Lenny Lind, CoVision

Pre-Reads Combined With Creative Questions

Give provocation *before* people are in the room and then refer to it when the group is together. "What do you see as the critical issue that we need to address?" or "What are some questions that you would love to see addressed in this meeting?" and use as kickoff for small group activity or during introduction.

— Anthony Weeks, Graphic Recorder

ENTERING

Fun Name Badges

Besides making it easy to read, let people customize their name badges with things like colored markers, stickers, glitter. In workshops that Innovation Games founder Luke Hohmann conducts, these materials are on each table. Participants found themselves enhancing their name tents over the duration of the two-day workshop, and the creations were very much a reflection of the person.

— Luke Hohmann, Innovation Games

A4/Letter-Sized Badge for Posting

Each person is invited to take a large sheet of paper and write their name, company and draw a picture of their face (sometimes this can be prepared in advance with a photo included). Participants are then invited to write things like favorite phrase or quote or expectations for the meeting. These cards are then hung on a large banner to share with others or as a sign of commitment.

— Sara Seravalle, SketchApensieri, Italy

Reception Showcase

The evening before the conference began, delegates were invited to attend a networking reception. The foyer was used to create a visual showcase of achievements. A series of eight 4'x 8' custom charts were created in advance and displayed throughout the reception area. The charts included information about several initiatives, the conference goals and a visual agenda. This engaged participants immediately as they entered the event and provided interesting things to view and spark meaningful conversations.

Options for expanding this idea include posting paper or stacks of sticky notes nearby so people can comment, as well as providing takeaway versions for delegates.

— Lisa Arora, Get The Picture

Create an Air of Anticipation and Welcome through Invitation

When people arrive, leave them a letter of welcome with bottle of wine in hotel room, or food associated with the conference theme and they will think, "Wow, they really want me here!"

— Avril Orloff, Outside the Lines

Chapter 6: Once They Appear

I had contacted the conference keynote speaker before we arrived to see what information I could get about the presentation, but apparently he was still working on his slides and said he would send them to me "soon." I didn't receive anything, so I sent another email before flying to the location, asking if he had them ready. "No," was the email response; he was still "tweaking a few slides."

I got to the large conference room early so I could set up and meet the speaker. I walked up to him, once my paper was up on the wall, to introduce myself and ask again about the presentation. He was flustered, as he had just gotten to the room, was trying to figure out the remote, and was still fussing with one or two slides. I finally gave up and decided that I would just hear it and capture it when the speaker delivered his talk. Needless to say, it didn't go well.

This example shows bad planning on two sides: the presentation and the whole conference structure. No one should have to sit though that kind of speaker and, why hadn't the event organizers insisted he was prepared well in advance?

Let's revisit the START Meeting Model.

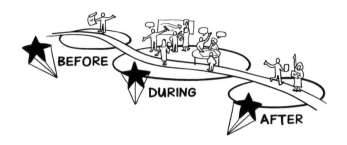

We have entered the DURING phase. So, we need to make sure that when we are thinking about what happens at the meeting, we have anticipated—BEFORE—the needs and goals of the participants. We structure the meeting so that we hit all six parts of the DURING phase.

THE IDEAL CONFERENCE

Not too long ago, I was talking to a friend who reminded me that MOST conferences are not at all like the conferences I work on, where visual and creative elements are embedded in some form or another, where the designers think about the food, the networking, the opportunities for genuine conversations, and where the options for storytelling abound. Most conferences are 45 minutes of a speaker presentation (and 100 PowerPoint slides of words and charts), followed by another 45 minutes of a speaker presentation (and 100 PowerPoint slides of words and charts), then a coffee break, and then? Another speaker. You get the picture.

I know that these awful meetings and conferences exist. I hear about them through friends. I walk by them on my way to lunch. Those poor people! How can conference organizers and leaders inflict this inhumane form of torture on others? Don't they know what it feels like to be in the audience? And many of those same audience members would willingly get up and torment their colleagues the same way. They just don't know any better!

When I start talking about how events could be greatly improved through some planning, creativity, and imagination, people become intrigued. I can almost see their thought bubbles: "Is she talking science fiction?"

Imagine this: Arriving at a conference, already intrigued by teaser campaigns that have started to get attendees thinking about what they'd like to learn, know, or better understand. Bags are given out upon registration that contain materials related to the subject, perhaps games or activities that have prizes for the winner. There is information on how to connect with other attendees and how to access content that is created or shared at the meeting. URLs are provided to access the visual maps being created on-site or to a Twitter feed curated for participants, encouraging you to get involved and share your ideas. Speakers have you captivated and even involve you in the conversation. You have ample time to discuss all the new ideas you've accrued with the people you've met. After the conference there is still a connection technologically, intellectually, socially, and visually.

PARTICIPATING

It may not seem like a huge thing, but I can tell what kind of conference it is by looking at the chairs. I shudder when I see the classroom set-up of chairs facing the front, or round tables crowded with chairs.

> "The chair tells you what kind of meeting it will be."

—Greg Bogue, Experience Architect, Maritz Travel

Creating spaces for participation and engagement is one of the ways to invite your attendees to get involved.

Gail Taylor, Co-founder of MGTaylor Corporation (with husband, Matt Taylor) and, more recently, Founder and Chairman of Tomorrow Makers—a consulting firm dedicated to teaching and stewarding collaboration—says this about the meeting space itself:

> To us, the space has to be kinesthetic. There have to be things that people must do. They must stand up and work with each other. They cannot sit around a table and work in any kind of way. I mean, that may be one module, but mostly—we've had whole design shops where people never sit down.

The risk you take is how do you create a sense of play? How do you create an environment that invites originality, spontaneity, in the moment? And I know it's difficult at conferences, but, after doing it with the World Economic Forum, then we got to do more and more.

If, in fact, they really want to help with collaboration, it's to recognize that each of us is unique and individual, and we have our different ways of learning and knowing. And if we really want that, then we have to honor the different intelligences in any session (whether it'd be thirty minutes, or any session wanting something from the group). There are thirty-minute meetings where it's a check-in, and that's the purpose. There are lots of project meetings that don't need this (but then consider the different intelligences and how are those people going to find their way and trust in themselves and others).

So let's take a look at the largest single focus of most conferences as a way to understand how to START Meeting the way we want—inspired and engaged.

NETWORKING

There are so many ways to make sure your participants network with each other you will have no problem finding a way to get them involved.

In fact, based on the idea that networking is one of only two reasons why they come to your event, it takes some work to stop them. People manage to create meetings where interaction is shut down, but it's easier and better when you create the space for getting to know each other.

- Allow downtime for people to interact and have conversations.
- Create fun spaces to sit and mingle. At *Wisdom 2.0*, Google sponsored an area that had beanbags, colorful rugs, and comfortable couches.
- Give people tools that kick start conversations e.g., name badges that say where they're from or a hobby they have.

EXPERIENTIAL LEARNING

Presenters and speakers take up a huge amount of the time in a meeting or conference. Upping the quality and kind of speaking experience can immediately change your event for the better. This is what your participants are living through. Make it come alive for them.

> "People can LISTEN, or MAKE MEANING, but not at the same time."

— Lisa Arora, Founder and Principal, Get The Picture

Ever had the feeling that the speaker was looking at their material almost for the first time themselves? It sure doesn't build audience confidence that the speaker was prepared or had rehearsed their talk, let alone that they cared if they came off as a subject matter expert. And when the slides are poorly done, you really get a sense that they could have sent a document out or provided a handout, instead of standing and torturing an audience with bad slides.

Hayley Foster, a Short Talk Expert, professional speaker, and the author of *Don't Tank Your TED Talk*, coaches speakers on how to wow the audience by honing in on the key message, illustrating with stories distilled to their essence. Here is her list of tips and tricks for giving the attendees what they came for.

Great Talks

- Condensed to 20 minutes and under.
- Contains a single core message.
- Speaker is the vehicle for the message, not the other way around.
- Be authentic.
- Use storytelling to connect to the listener.
- Clear visuals.

- No painful slide deck.
- Involve the audience.
- Relevant to the audience.
- Know the talk well without seeming over rehearsed.
- Practice in front of real people.
- Leaves the listener with an emotional connection to the material.

The presenter's performance can be improved by creating slides that engage the audience rather than bore them to tears, as Nancy Duarte, Principal of Duarte Design, does. Duarte believes that an image can speak volumes about the speaker's content, and is certainly more appealing than a slide full of unreadable content. Speaker coaching can help presenters to create a powerful but concise message, as Foster does as a Short Talk Expert. Foster works with speakers to create punchy talks that concisely move an audience using powerful stories and messages. TED, and more popularized TEDx local events, use an amazing format where speakers provide leading-edge insights, or as TED calls them, "Ideas worth spreading."

One of the reasons the talks are so good is that the TED organizers provide the presenters with ten speaking guidelines.

The "TED Commandments"

1. Thou Shalt Not Simply Trot Out Thy Usual Shtick.
2. Thou Shalt Dream a Great Dream, or Show Forth a Wondrous New Thing, Or Share Something Thou Hast Never Shared Before.
3. Thou Shalt Reveal Thy Curiosity and Thy Passion.
4. Thou Shalt Tell a Story.
5. Thou Shalt Freely Comment on the Utterances of Other Speakers for the Sake of Blessed Connection and Exquisite Controversy.
6. Thou Shalt Not Flaunt Thine Ego. Be Thou Vulnerable. Speak of Thy Failure as well as Thy Success.
7. Thou Shalt Not Sell from the Stage: Neither Thy Company, Thy Goods, Thy Writings, nor Thy Desperate Need for Funding; Lest Thou be Cast Aside into Outer Darkness.
8. Thou Shalt Remember All the While: Laughter is Good.
9. Thou Shalt Not Read Thy Speech.
10. Thou Shalt Not Steal the Time of Them that Follow Thee.

Author Daniel Pink offers these three key tips:

1. Prepare . . . but not too much.

These days, very few TED speakers arrive unprepared and just try to wing their presentations. That's great. Preparing is a sign of respect for your audience—and the only way to wrangle your ideas inside an eighteen or nine-minute fence. But lately I've seen a handful of people who were *too* prepared and *too* rehearsed. Their presentations were so heavily shellacked that they seemed inauthentic; their ideas suffocated under all that varnish. Remember: Human beings, despite their imperfections (and sometimes *because* of their imperfections), are far more persuasive than expertly tuned presentation robots.

2. Say something important.

There's a big difference between saying some important things and saying something important. Your goal isn't to demonstrate how much you know or to catalog your many insights, but to leave the audience with one idea to ponder—or better, one step to take. When people hear some important things, their heads nod. When they hear something important, their souls stir, their brains engage, and their bodies prepare to act.

> "ALL OF US ARE NATURALLY BORN STORYTELLERS"
>
> — Nancy Duarte,
> Principal,
> Duarte Design

> "In the next decade, it will become more important than ever to move from simply gaining people's attention to engaging them in more participatory and interactive experiences."

— Institute for the Future

3. Say it like yourself.

Don't mimic someone else's style or conform to what you think is a particular "TED way" of presenting. That's boring, banal, and backward. Don't try to be the next Ken Robinson or the next Jill Bolte Taylor. Be the first you.

SHARING/COMMUNICATING

The speakers' presentations are just part of the event experience for a participant. From the moment that people arrive at the event, there should be ways to meet their two primary needs. Here they are again:

1. To learn NEW leading-edge insights.
2. To meet NEW people.

Think of it: how can you encourage people to learn once they've shown up? How can you improve the overall experience so it's fun? How can you create an atmosphere that encourages networking? And how can you help with the digestion and integration of experiences, conversations, and discussions—not to mention implementation of these NEW ideas and follow-up with these NEW people?

The first need, learning, can be expanded to include a way to engage with both the content and the other participants. This is where visual methodologies really can play an important part in creating a great conference experience. There are great techniques that can be used in keynote sessions and breakout sessions, and there are also ways to engage people with each other and the key topics between sessions.

Try getting rid of the tables. Tables allow people to emotionally hide behind a physical barrier. Try small group conversation, or a World Café Style talk. One of my clients set up the entire conference room with beanbag chairs. They moved around easily (which helped with breakout sessions), they were fun, and they broke down barriers. One simple change threw everyone into new ways of thinking and interaction. Take a look at the Best Practices section for ways to introduce more sharing and communicating in your meetings.

STORYTELLING

Storytelling is not only a subset of communication, or a way of learning, it is how our brains are wired. Books are popping up everywhere to train leaders to be good storytellers, to explain why our brains run on a story, to help you use a story to sell an idea. You can easily bring STORYTELLING into your meetings.

> **"Stories tell us what we already knew and forgot, and remind us of what we haven't yet imagined."**

— Anne Watson, Author and Storyteller

I am not talking fiction and other experts back me up. Michelle Auerbach, a novelist, writer for the *New York Times*, and an Organizational Storytelling Consultant, explains it like this, "Story is the absolute best way to get across any information, motivate people to act, get an audience involved, or hold interest in otherwise boring topics. Our brains use story to carry

emotion and aid in memory. Bringing simple storytelling techniques into your meeting is a way to ensure that people will remember the information and bring it back home with them."

"Some people think we're made of flesh and blood and bone. Scientists say we're made of atoms. But I think we're made of stories! When we die, that's what people remember, the stories of our lives and the stories we told."

— Ruth Stotter, Author and Storyteller

Storytelling can be visual, it can be in a video, it can be written, but we all know it when we see it. Auerbach explains it like this, "You know a story because it has an arc. Something changes in the course of it. There is a build up of tension and a release. And you feel differently at the end than you did at the beginning. That tension and release and the change makes neurochemical changes happen in your brain. It draws you in and makes the meeting come alive." Story could be a PowerPoint presentation on how meeting sales goals will change the ability of the business to do other great work. It could be a speaker telling an authentic moment from their lives that

led to their career. It could be the opportunity for participants to talk to each other about why they are at the conference in the first place. In fact, having the participants tell stories to each other accomplishes almost all the goals of the DURING phase of the START Meeting Model.

According to Anthony Weeks, graphic recorder, visual storyteller, and information designer, "You can create graphic charts for those in the room, and then make sure the participants can use them to tell the stories of the meeting to people who were not there. The participants can tell their own story of the meeting from the charts, and that creates repeatable internalized experience that people are excited about." He goes on to remind us, "good stories will bring data to life." It makes the data real, comprehensible, and memorable.

The challenge: How do we turn DATA into STORIES? Weeks points out some key thoughts:

- We are often talked *to* vis a vis PowerPoints with lots of data, lots of slides, and it's obvious that lots of research has gone into it and you've done your due diligence, but no matter how well it's presented, WHO CARES if you can't tell the story. There needs to be a balance between data and story.
- We now have an obsession with BIG DATA, and yet this makes it even more important to be able to distill the information down or you overwhelm people.

- We prioritize what we make time for; it's crucial at the end of presentations to make space to create stories that are repeatable, memorable and spark further conversations.

- Bob Johansen, CEO of The Institute for the Future (IFTF) in Palo Alto, California and author of *Get There Early*, often riffs on a practice generated by Columbia Business School Professor, Willie Pieterson, where he moves away from the quantitative "value proposition" instead to a "winning proposition," forcing people to describe how they will do what they do BETTER than others for their customers and deliver significant financial value for themselves—what are you actually going to DO? He asks them to create a story of what it looks like, and does not let them use words like "enable" and "advance" that have no true meaning.

- Where there is a graphic, Johansen invites people to come up and, using the chart, lead the group through their winning proposition in a way that is interesting and compelling. They find that in the first round, people just read what's on the chart, but over time, they learn to improvise and tell their own story, even embellishing it with their own narrative. This practice tests to see if there is a story as well as where the gaps are. It helps transfer storytelling capability and through repetitive success of telling the story again and again, people get more comfortable with the format.

- Storytelling creates intrigue, invites questions, invites dialogue . . . "What do you want to know?"

ACTION PLANNING

Let's go back to why people come to conferences. We have talked quite a bit about the interaction, but there is also the desire to learn something new and to come into contact with new ideas. There is an old adage that we retain approximately ten percent of what we see; thirty to forty percent of what we see and hear; and ninety percent of what we see, hear, and do. So make sure to include all of the learning styles: visual, auditory, and kinesthetic to make sure you meet the goals of your entire audience.

Dr. Medina would argue that hands down, we are all visual learners:

we think in pictures and need to create vivid mental images. We enjoy looking at charts, pictures, and videos. But, some people do require additional senses to be engaged in order to really grasp and learn.

Auditory learners learn via listening. They learn through discussions and think in words rather than pictures. Kinesthetic learners learn by doing things and touching them. They have a hard time sitting still and may become distracted. If you want more information, this is expanded on in David Kolb's Experiential Learning Model.

On average, studies have shown that roughly:

- 29% of the population has a visual preference.
- 34% has an auditory preference.
- 37% have a kinesthetic preference.

At the end of an event, it's important that people figure out what they are going to do as a result of new knowledge, skills, or interactions. Follow up can be challenging, but so important to do before people drift back into their normal routines.

How can you help make an impact?

Again, it's about creating space for action planning to happen; to help people with a structure for things they want to walk away with. Some ideas include:

- What are the top three ideas I learned that I want to share with colleagues?
- What are the three actions I will take to move these strategies forward?
- Who are three people I met at this event that I will connect with within one month?

Writing these down can be powerful and help with retention. Even more powerful is giving people an opportunity to share them aloud. Another

strong way to create commitment is to publicly sign something, whether it's a Vision Statement, or a commitment to action. These can be photographed and reproduced and made available to everyone after the event as a reminder.

I will never forget an event where my team of ten graphic recorders worked tirelessly for four days, visually capturing content during plenary sessions and then working with regional breakout teams. At the end of the week, when we did a "Gallery Walk," each participant was given a sheet of paper as they entered the walk. On it, they were asked to note highlights and key points from the charts. Next, the large group was convened and invited to share their insights. Using their notes, they shared things that had come from the events of the week. The comment that brought a tear to my eye was from one person who stood and said, "In the past, we raced around taking pictures of all the flip charts, because we knew the information would disappear soon after the conference. Now, we have beautiful charts that are digitally captured for us so we can learn, reference, and share them with others. Thank you."

No, Thank YOU.

Ask anyone and they'll tell you this: engage multiple senses and you have a much better chance of making your point and having it remembered.

SUMMARY

During a meeting, the START Meeting Model gives us six ways to up the interaction, engagement, and satisfaction of the participants. These are: Participating, Networking, Experiential Learning, Sharing/Communicating, Storytelling, and Action Planning. If you can help your speakers understand their role, and address the different learning styles of your attendees, you can create an incredible experience during your meeting. And if you can create engagement with the participants to do something as a result, you've hit a home run.

Chapter 7: During - Best Practices

In this section of Best Practices, you will find hands-on ways to incorporate the START Meeting Model into any meeting, event, or conference you are planning. You can pick and choose among the ideas for whatever phase of the START Meeting Model you want to strengthen your meetings. You can combine them, adapt them to your circumstances, expand them, or make up your own. If you find something that works especially well, make sure to email us and let us know what you did and how it worked. Creating inspiring events is a creative and evolving process, and you are cordially invited to share it with us.

QUICK IDEAS . . .

- Get rid of the tables whenever you can!
- Use music to set the tone, bring people back from breaks and energize.
- Help people to break out of conditioned power structures.
- Get outside! Use the entire space you have and help people to move out of a corporate mindset.
- Use graphic recorders and others as roving reporters, wandering and listening during breakouts with notepads as they capture the essence of the conversations.
- Get people out of their chairs, moving around and interacting.

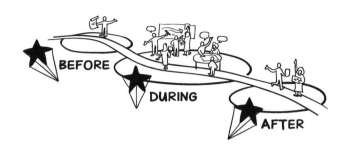

PARTICIPATING

Roxanne

Using the song, tell half the group (have them count off or just divide the room) that they will jump to the RIGHT when they hear the word "Roxanne," and the other half of the group will jump to the LEFT when they hear the words "Red Light." Try it yourself and then imagine a whole group doing this.

— Patrick Marr, The Leading Edge

Take a Panel

Give each person a panel, whether it be a poster board or flip chart sheet, and using markers, have them write their views on a particular subject or answer a few questions. The process of writing helps to bring individuals into a group.

— Sita Magnuson, depict llc

Graffiti Wall

Create a large wall chart beforehand with a fun graphic frame that looks a bit like graffiti. The format is inviting for participants to respond to a question(s) by writing, in words and pictures, on the chart with markers. Place the chart where

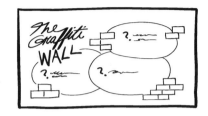

participants will walk by with instructions of what to do. If possible, have someone by the chart to "invite" people to contribute, especially early on. This can be used to get people talking about a topic or get a sense of what people are thinking about, concerned about or excited about.

— Dana Wright, Take Action Inc.

Kick-Off Question Capture

During introduction or even using just a chart to capture, write (or they can write on large sticky notes) participant answers to a question that they may have been given in advance of the meeting. This is better shared out loud so people can hear the thoughts of others, as it can reinforce views held by multiple people.

— Anthony Weeks, Graphic Recorder

Opening with Hopes and Fears

Beginning a meeting by asking each person to share their hopes for the event, their fears for the event—either or both, and capturing these comments on a board to be referenced back throughout the meeting.

— Dana Wright, Take Action Inc.

NETWORKING

Have You Ever . . . (Like Musical Chairs)

Give each person a small piece of tape and have them stand and form a circle. Stand in the center of the circle and have each person place their piece of tape under their feet. Tell them that when they are in the center, they will say something that they've done (e.g., traveled to Europe, been on a roller coaster, tried sushi), in the hopes that others will have also done what they say. If you have, for example, traveled to Europe, then you must move to a different spot in the circle. The person in the center will go to an open spot, which will force someone else to move into the center (not the desired spot!). This person will find a different question that will create movement. This is a great way to learn things about your team!

— Dana Wright, Take Action Inc. (I credit a client at Banfield Pet Hospital for this activity.)

Hand Tracing

At meetings John facilitates, he will have a large sheet of paper on the wall with colored, scented markers available. His instructions are: trace your dominant hand with your non-dominant hand (hint: this makes all the tracings look very youthful). When finished, write your name and the very first thing you can remember you wanted to be when you grew up. He

then facilitates a conversation by inviting each person to share their story. It's always interesting to hear what childhood dreams people had.

— Dana Wright, Take Action Inc. (I credit John Williams, Woomera Group.)

Engagement Speed Dating

Similar to romantic speed dating, yet the questions are a bit more meeting focused. Ask one of the following questions and have everyone in the room find a partner and share their answers. Timing should be quick. Ask another question and have them find a new partner to share answers. Some questions can be:

- What did you enjoy most about yesterday?
- What are you excited about today?
- When were you most engaged in your career and what was it like?
- What challenge do you hope to find a solution for today?

— Patrick Marr, The Leading Edge

Gifts Exercise

Based on work by Peter Block, each person puts their name at the top of a blank sheet of paper. They then write numbers down the page that total the number of people in the room, not including themselves. The paper is passed to the right (or left) and this person writes, at the top spot, a gift that person whose name appears at the top brings to the team (this activity requires the group know each other). The paper rotation continues in the same direction until everyone has had a chance to recognize a gift for

everyone else on the team. At the end, the original person gets the completed sheet as a memento of what the others appreciate about them.

— Jen Schulte, Mars Incorporated

Picnic Lunch Meet and Greet

At a TEDx event, picnic baskets containing lunch items for six people each were distributed on blankets around a site. Participants were invited to find five other people they didn't know and sit together over lunch, sharing their meal as well as their experiences.

— Hayley Foster, Short Talk Expert

EXPERIENTIAL LEARNING

Speed Networking

Similar to speed dating, create three-minute rotations to discuss thoughts and reactions to content of a presentation, for example, "What have you learned about strategic partnerships since we last met?"

— Nevada Lane, Lane Change Consulting

Partner Walks

Another way to help participants assimilate what they've heard, discuss thoughts and reactions to content is to allow time for pairs to take a walk, giving them a focus question, sometimes along with a small index card to take visual notes.

— Nevada Lane, Lane Change Consulting

Presenter Fishbowls

As an alternative to having a panel of presenters, consider having a circle of presenters, surrounded by a circle of participants. The advantage is that the participants' mindsets are shifted by a different style of presentation and setup, resulting in better listening (think about it-you are sitting across from people who can see your face, as opposed to being one darkly lit face in an audience all facing forward).

— Nevada Lane, Lane Change Consulting

Fruits of Wisdom

Using a large, hand-drawn tree with many branches, participants are invited to write on apple-shaped stickies (find these on Amazon) where they can write some of the "fruits" of the workshop and attach them to the tree.

— Brenda Tan-See Lay Hua, Trailblazer Associates, Singapore

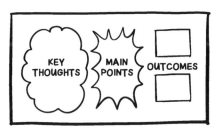

Learning Template

A visual template is created with space specifically labeled with event topics to capture high-level learning and key points over the course of the event.

— Jolynn Chow, Beyond Words Training, Singapore

Incorporate Social Responsibility Principles

Part of our corporate value system is to not just be takers in the world, but to: 1) Do good, 2) Be good citizens, and 3) Help the local community. With that in mind, we try to find local causes in the areas we hold our events that we can contribute to. In Mexico, for example, we found out that many men move their families far away  and they have no social support. A group of woman had an organization where they sell things they made (dolls, bags) as a way to contribute to the family income. We brought them to our event to sell their beautiful items. In addition, we created a team building event using canned goods that we donated to a local organization. We also asked people to bring gently used clothing to the offsite, which could then be donated.

— Stephen Zaruba & John Quereto, Expressworks

Unique Spaces and Environment

Sometimes we're confined to the spaces we get, but it's really fun to design amazing and creative spaces to get the best out of the participants. In one two-day session, we worked with a communications company in the UK.  They created an indoor beach experience, with breakout stations set up in sand. There were beach chairs to sit in, clothes lines to hang flip chart paper, coolers with drinks and wood slat walls to generate ideas. An ideation session was held in Easton, Pennsylvania at the Crayola Factory, where

color and creativity abound, the warm and waxy scent of crayons brings you back to childhood. The knOwhere Store builds custom environments that allow for creativity, collaboration and engagement. Any space that allows people to wander around, touch things, play with things and explore. "In order to get the best out of people, you need to create the space for this to happen."

— Anthony Weeks (quote), Graphic Recorder and Dana Wright, Take Action Inc.

Local Experiences

When an event is located out of town for participants, it's great to somehow fold in an activity that gets people outside and experiencing the location. You can design activities like scavenger hunts, geocaching, or progressive events—even meals can be done this way! At one event, we were in Amsterdam and as we rode in our boat in the canal, we stopped at three different ports and picked up different courses to our dinner!

— Dana Wright, Take Action Inc.

Collaborative Drawing

Divide groups into smaller groups, give them a question and have them draw collaboratively. Get them started by one person making a mark or shape—can be anything, just not a word. Go around the room and have each person add something. The caveat? They are working in silence, until

everyone has had a chance to participate. Then they can talk about the key aspects of their drawings. Debrief is a sharing of the experience; often find it allows for a different understanding because the activity did not involve words and conversation. The power of NOT knowing and what will emerge.

— Avril Orloff, Outside the Lines

SHARING/COMMUNICATING

Conversation Table Templates

There are so many ways to use templates during events as a way to focus discussions and reflect on what's been heard. Often, what's needed is simply a way to digest what has just been presented. A few questions for table templates could be:

- What SURPRISED you?
- What CHALLENGED you?
- What INSPIRED you?
  — Dana Wright, Take Action Inc.

Conversation Wall Templates

Similar to the table templates, these structured templates create a space for people to contribute their thoughts during an event. What's great about a template is that the brain wants it filled in, so participants are inspired to complete it. A few general questions might be:

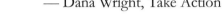

- What did you like BEST today?
- What could be done DIFFERENTLY?
- What did you LEARN?
- What CONCERNS do you have?

— Dana Wright, Take Action Inc.

Knowledge Wall

At an event, it's quite easy to get lost or overwhelmed at the amount of information that is coming at you. Adopted from MGTaylor, the practice is about creating a central place to get grounded. A visual frame is created before the event begins with the story of the event pre-populated visually. As the event unfolds, the wall (which are generally large sheets of foam board but can be paper, four feet wide by eight feet long) is added to with highlights of breakout work, as well as things that "everyone needs to know" or "gems to share." These can be photos or words, and can be written on stickies or various sizes of paper by participants or a graphic recorder.

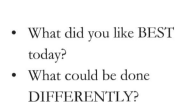
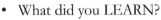
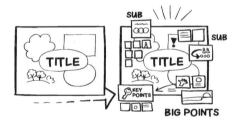

— Sita Magnuson, dpict llc

Idea Wall

Create a graphic frame at the start of the event, and invite participants to come up and write what inspired them, what value they've gotten from the workshops/talks/meetings/events over the course of the event and what they plan to do as a result.

— Sophia Liang, Graphic Footprints

Alternatives to Flip Chart Capture

Instead of using the standard flip chart easel, try something different. Imagine walking into a session and seeing chairs in circles with cardboard boxes (18x18x18) being used as the centerpiece (no table). The boxes are then used as writing surfaces, and when the small teams come together, they stack the boxes together as a way to share their ideas.

— Gail Taylor, Tomorrow Makers Inc.

Iterative Presentation and Interaction Structure

Present initial content, followed by group interaction to engage with what's been presented, then more content followed by more group interaction (versus fill you up in the morning with content, then asking for group interaction and planning after lunch…not the greatest time to get people's best thinking). The iterative process helps in assimilating content.

— Avril Orloff, Outside the Lines

Bean Bag Conversation

Using the beanbag as a prop to move the conversation, the group stands and forms a circle. The facilitator asks them a topic-related question. The first person with the beanbag answers the question, and then throws to someone else, who is required to start with "Yes, AND . . ." and then add their idea, and then pass the beanbag to someone else. So much more active and involved than a scribe at a flip chart!

— Avril Orloff, Outside the Lines

Gallery Walk

The first time I heard this term used was through The Grove Consultants International. This is the concept of putting all visuals created during an event on the walls or boards of some sort and displaying them in order of creation. One client set up the large ballroom as a park scene, complete with potted trees and park benches. As each person entered the room, they were given a handout that asked them to capture three key learnings, best ideas or top takeaways as they walked around the room.

— Anthony Weeks, Graphic Recorder and Tim Hamons, Singapore

STORYTELLING

Graphic Timeline

Create a timeline or spectrum of some sort and invite people to put themselves on the chart in some way, either by writing or using sticky notes. (Neuland sells these in the shape of people.) The timeline can be based on when they started with the organization or industry or any other meaningful dimension.

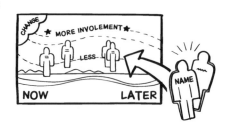

— Emily Shepard, The Graphic Distillery

Key Word Template

A more challenging but amazing visual is created when one key word is created on a large mural in huge block letters; a graphic recorder then captures the major concepts within these letters and uses color around the letters to make them pop. Some banners can be scattered around the chart as subtitles.

— Anna-Lena Schiller, Hamburg, Germany

Team Engagement Vision

Start with blank business cards or small pieces of paper, given to each participant. Instruct them to quickly answer a question, such as "Engagement is…". Working in pairs, have them each share their definition and then agree on one definition. Next, combine them with another pair and again share and agree one definition. This may take several iterations, depending on group size, but in the end, the entire group pulls together to align on one common definition—this will take some facilitation and word-smithing but worth it.

— Jen Schulte, Mars Incorporated

Picture the Vision

Invite participants to use one piece of paper, landscape format, to draw the current state of their team, organization or industry and another sheet, again landscape format, to draw the aspirational/future state. Encourage them to use words and pictures in their drawings and when finished, post them on two separate boards. This often helps show the stress and chaos of the current state. Sometimes I will use the Center for Creative Leadership's "Visual Explorer" cards, which have interesting photographs for this purpose, yet a bit less personal.

— Emily Shepard, The Graphic Distillery and Dana Wright, Take Action Inc.

Poster Formatted Content Capture

TED-style events are quick and focused. One way to memorialize the content is to have a graphic recorder capture the key bullets on a poster-sized foam board set on an easel or flip chart stand. These can be very colorful and bright. Australian colleague Gavin Blake likes to bring an assistant along and while he captures the content using black only, his assistant takes a photograph, digitizes it and colors them in Photoshop. At the end of the day, all the boards are complete. Often these boards can be displayed on breaks in "towers," where three board are taped together to form triangles, and the triangles can then be stacked, creating a very powerful visual display for participants.

— Gavin Blake, Fever Picture, Australia and Wyn Wilson, Graphic Recorders

ACTION PLANNING

Commitment Cards

Something as simple as commitment cards could be distributed to participants, with a provocative question or space for "Key points I want to remember" or "Three actions I plan to take back at the office." These

can be shared out loud (which solidifies the commitment), collected, and summarized or just held individually as a reminder.

— Dana Wright, Take Action Inc.

Self-Written Commitment Postcards

People make commitments during a meeting of things they will do once they return to work. These commitments are often mixed with the rest of the meeting notes, thus lost and forgotten soon afterward. Have a prepared postcard, with either the conference logo or a graphic of some sort made up ahead of time with postage included, so the commitments can be written on the reverse side, and simply addressed back to the participant.

— Dana Wright, Take Action Inc.

Commitment Wall

It is very powerful to have a group sign an image that represents the work they've done during an event. Sometimes this is an agreement, a vision or an action plan. This can be photographed or scanned and then sent to each participant as a reminder.

— Emily Shepard, The Graphic Distillery

Commitment Poster

It's very powerful to create a large visual of a vision or strategy and then have each participant sign it. This can later be scanned and distributed to each person. In one instance, the vision was hand-painted on to a framed canvas, and at the end of the meeting, after many interactive sessions to understand the direction and opportunity to give input and ask questions, each person was invited to sign the canvas. This framed poster was then displayed in the headquarters building.

— Dana Wright, Take Action Inc.

Chapter 8: Making It Last

I had just finished facilitating at a big five-day meeting on Italy's northern coast (also known as the Italian Riviera). It was late June, and the sun shone brightly on the Ligurian Sea. We were all staying at the magnificent Excelsior Palace Hotel, right on the harbor.

The conference was a gathering of sixty-five internal HR leaders from a multi-national corporation to talk about their vision for the next five years and strategies to get there. During the week, time was devoted to talking about leadership. The Vice President of HR talked about his personal framework: "Having the geese fly in formation" (we would make jokes about these geese for many years to come).

Many formal presentations were followed by breakout sessions to discuss the strategies and concepts presented. The week culminated in one of the most memorable evening events I can remember attending with a client. It was held at a restaurant called U Giancu's Restaurant, owned by an American cartoon aficionado, with wine tasting and hors d'oeuvres, followed by a tasty dinner, limoncello (Italian lemon liqueur), and a great American band playing a range of popular music. The entire group danced, sang, and danced some more in the hills above Rapallo.

On Friday at 5:00 pm, the meeting concluded and the final participant left the meeting room. As I sat on the floor rolling finished charts, I had this strange sense: where did everyone go? I suddenly found it so sad

to go from being on and engaged with the group to suddenly being off and finished.

Let's revisit the START Meeting Model.

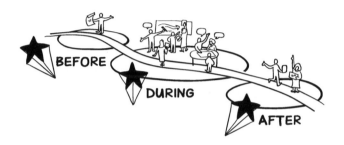

AFTERGLOW - OR NOT

Most people are so anxious to leave conferences and get on the road afterward, either literally or by air, and get to their next engagement (home or work) that they start to disengage well before the event officially ends. The idea of spending time thinking about what was learned, both in each session and the overall learnings, is rarely considered. Often, there's little to no thought given to how the information may impact oneself and others (okay, maybe a passing thought), but certainly no concerted effort is made to do anything about it.

After I attend a conference as a participant, I carefully store all my best notes, and I put the audiotapes (or MP3 files) on a shelf, with a sincere intention to revisit them… "at some point." Occasionally, because I'm a very good note taker, I'll go back to my notes to find a specific piece of information I remember. But then, I carefully put the notebook back where it was—gathering dust.

Of course, logic tells me that if I took that notebook out and re-read my own notes, or better yet, talked them over with someone else, I could remember them better and possibly utilize what I learned. I have the best of intentions. Suddenly, it's six months later and I haven't done anything with my new knowledge, not even shared it with someone else. *Can you relate to this?*

Some would argue that it's not such a big deal. Which drives the point: If you forget everything within ninety days, are you really getting the return on your investment that you expected? Whether you're an attendee or an employer, whether you're a facilitator or a speaker, whether you're a conference planner or organizer, you want the value of the event to persist as far and as long as possible. I met one woman in Joplin, Missouri who said, "If I come back with a single idea, my boss considers it a success."

You need to aim much higher than that.

What could be done to create a different outcome?

There are two parts to the After phase of a meeting in the START Meeting Model. There is Leaving and Extending. Leaving is being deliberate in the way you end a meeting, how you say goodbye, that you have a close to your meeting. Extending is making sure your meeting stays in people's heads and that they are engaged with the content and the speakers and their information long after the event is over.

LEAVING

In smaller retreats, I've seen time at the end of meetings dedicated to summarizing the key points that came out of each agenda item. When summarized and distributed, it becomes a group memory rather than counting on each individual to remember the events the same way. This is particularly important when you're counting on participants to carry back the content and messages to others effectively.

Even better: take these notes and make them visual in some way, so participants and those they share the information with can see how things fit together and can view the path to get from one point to the next. In working with one client, we collected these ideas and created both a summary graphic and a slide deck, which took apart each element of the graphic and explained each one in more detail. Once you understand how the parts fit together, the big picture makes more sense.

If you have graphic maps of your meeting, a Gallery Walk where participants pair up and walk through the event together reminiscing and telling stories about the parts that were most impactful is a way to end a meeting with storytelling.

Greg Bogue, Experience Architect at Maritz Travel, told a story about one memorable meeting ending: "They had their key executives be at the bus at the airport upon departure date, shake hands and tell people thank you." You can bet that every person who attended that meeting remembered the moment they were met at the bus by their leaders and thanked. It put a perfect end to their time together.

EXTENDING

Avril Orloff, a Graphic Recorder at Outside the Lines, says, "People blow their budget on the event itself. People think in limited ways and don't continue the dialogue, and if it's an annual event, it's like you get people very excited and engaged and then you give them NOTHING afterward-deflating their balloon, so you start over each year. 'Conversationalis Interruptus'—if you don't capitalize on the momentum, you lose some of their energy for the next year."

Avoid the Conversationalis Interruptus at all costs. Plan in advance for how the ideas will flow and what will happen after the meeting.

> - In the planning phase, consider ways to make the information last, be accessed, and communicated
> - Determine what are the key ideas you want people to walk away knowing and remembering
> - Establish how you'll reinforce these messages throughout the event
> - Make sure to plan for how to keep engagement after the event

Time also has to be carved out during the conference for attendees to make sense of all they're hearing and to make connections between different pieces of data during the event itself. You can't always count on people to do this for themselves. Creating forums specifically for supporting this is useful, as people need some structure and the time set aside to do this type of synthesizing and integrating.

STORYBOOKS

After the event is over, materials that help participants process all they heard are very much appreciated. Often, we will create what's referred to as storybooks, which are a visual summary of the event. They include all the

graphically recorded charts (in order of appearance), along with annotations. At the front, there is a page that lists the objectives of the session, along with a list of attendees (for internal company sessions), list of presenters, and key guest appearances.

We will often include candid pictures, almost yearbook style, which engage people at another level and remind them of the event's atmosphere, energy, and outcomes. And people LOVE these books! Harkening back to their high school yearbook days, they anxiously page through, looking for familiar faces, then check out the charts from sessions during the week.

Janine Underhill and Michelle Auerbach work together at Amplify the Impact to create high production value visual and narrative storybooks for meetings and events utilizing the latest in brain science to drive the layout, narrative arc, and structure of the books. "We 'Amplify the Impact' of meetings through 'redintigration'. That's a fancy cognitive psychology word for using everyday events to bring back the whole event from memory. So we put the books together in ways that will spark memory and excitement." Underhill explains, "we also give participants a chance to become storytellers and bring the event to life for people who were not there. Organizations are recognizing the need to make their people storytellers. We all know how to tell a story from a storybook, so we give them the tools to go out and raise the roof on the meeting's ROI by bringing it to life over and over."

GRAPHIC ROADMAP

During one recent conference, we tracked the overall key points, along with speakers' highlights, evening events, and some great, memorable quotes into one big graphic roadmap for the entire event. In the evenings, a small sub-team of us created a visual summary of the four-day event using both words and graphics. (NOTE: Our graphic facilitation team had a BLAST during these nighttime sessions. While there were only three - four of us actually drawing the chart, all ten of us joined the fun, helping with content and laughing into the night). We were engaged and we were only the recorders, imagine the delight when the participants saw the map. Imagine still if they had engaged with it themselves.

The final chart, four feet wide by sixteen feet long, was revealed during a wrap-up session delivered by the CEO. Even though the audience couldn't see the details as the CEO used the chart to walk people through

their week, they knew it was accurate given their experience of our visual charts. In addition, they each received a page-sized (okay, supersized page) version of the chart after the event to review and reflect on. They were thrilled, and more than that, they remembered each event better having revisited them visually before they left.

What else could you do? You could engage the leaders and participants in video clips (during the conference and/or afterwards) to talk about different parts of the conference and then embed the clips in an electronic version of the chart. Also possible: mouse-overs of actual conference charts, links to presentations, and more candid photos from the week. And, I'm sure I'm just scratching the surface of what's possible. While we created the large summary chart throughout the conference, this also could have been created afterward with the same additions included.

ANIMATED VIDEOS

One of the hottest tools to share information or tell a story is the creation of graphic animated videos, many where words and pictures appear by a hand drawing (or no hand) while a voice narrates the content. Daniel Pink used RSA Animate to share content from his book *Drive* to talk about what motivates us. This video went viral on YouTube and suddenly everyone was doing these simple videos to promote a product, convey a concept, or share an idea. These animated whiteboard videos can be used effectively to cover conference themes, stories, messages and highlights.

MEETING IN A BOX

These are all interactive solutions, however there are some very basic ways to create engagement once the event is over. For example, a facilitator's guide for leading follow-up conversations can be created, sometimes called a Meeting in a Box. We once designed an Engagement Kit, which was a nice box with a conference logo that contained all the information to run a follow-up team session. We gave each person a flash drive that contained PDF's of templates to print as well as a Leader's Guide to help facilitate the conversation. These kits can be started (or possibly even finished) before the event begins. If there's a desire to bring in quotes from the event, these can be added in before distributing the guide for use or distributed later electronically.

THE PERFECT FOLLOW-UP

The key for any follow-up is for it to be done quickly and in the hands or view of participants immediately after the event. The longer the time delay, the more time for the memory of events to disappear. After two weeks, ninety percent of what is learned is lost. I've been part of a team

where we got storybooks into participants' hands before they even left the event. If you think about it, this is ideal: people have their whole commute time, back to reality, to review what they have just participated in before a new set of distractions arrive—which they will!

Here are a few more ideas to make the event last longer for participants:

- Presenters upload their slides to the event website shortly after the event, allowing the content to be fresh and accurate.
- Twitter streams help make event conversations last longer.
- Meetup allows you to upload photos from the event so people can associate a snapshot with a specific session or keynote.

YOU CAN TAKE IT WITH YOU

Brian Camastral, CEO of Riversong Sanctuary, Cofounder of BLITS Foundation, and former Global President of a large CPG company, gives two other great ideas from his meetings:

We had a website where every presentation that was filmed was available, and both the presentation and the video were available to use. All the visual captures [or graphic recordings] that were made were posted on the site, as well as the group output. Everybody was able to use the website materials simply to remember or to apply in their job or, ideally, to share.

Secondly, we created a toolkit. We then asked everyone who left there to cascade this into their own teams.

Gail Taylor, Co-founder of MGTaylor Corporation and Founder and Chairman of Tomorrow Markers, reaches out to participants after the fact. "We sometimes send out postcards with different graphics on them and different parts to different members and saying: 'Remember this?' or 'Call one of your colleagues today, share an idea.' "

SUMMARY

A few simple tools aid integration and learning. These tools can up the retention and engagement of your meeting. Plan up front what you want people to take away from the event. Make sure you give participants time at the end of the meeting to summarize what they have learned. Use visuals to bring back the story of the meeting like storybooks or slide decks

of the graphic maps created in the meeting. Give them something solid to use when they get home. And, keep in contact with them through email, Facebook, Twitter, LinkedIn or by helping them present their information once they get back.

Chapter 9: After - Best Practices

In this section of Best Practices, you will find hands-on ways to incorporate the START Meeting Model into any meeting, event, or conference you are planning. You can pick and choose among the ideas for whatever phase of the START Meeting Model you want to strengthen your meetings. You can combine them, adapt them to your circumstances, expand them, or make up your own. If you find something that works especially well, make sure to email us and let us know what you did and how it worked. Creating inspiring events is a creative and evolving process, and you are cordially invited to share it with us.

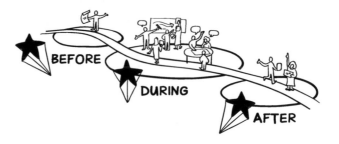

LEAVING

Summary Canvas

Using all the charts created at an event, a two-foot by three-foot canvas can be printed as a memento for attendees. The visuals provide a great way to jog participant's memories of the event and key points.

— Nevada Lane, Lane Change Consulting

Closing: One Word

Often I will end a meeting by asking people to share ONE WORD that encapsulates how they feel as a result of the meeting. By forcing people to narrow to one word, it creates focus and prevents a rambling conversation. If you're able, it's great to capture these words and then create a visual using Wordle or some other word cloud software.

— Dana Wright, Take Action Inc.

EXTENDING

Follow-Up Visual Postcards

Using the idea of "a picture is worth a thousand words," graphics from the event can be digitized and made into postcards (either a piece of a graphic, an entire graphic or all graphic charts with event information in the center), which are then mailed to participants with reminders of the event: quotes from speakers, key points, or a reminder of something the group committed to. You can even include a QR code that will link to video clips from the conference!

— Nevada Lane, Lane Change Consulting

One Page Summaries with Graphics and Speaker Notes

Using an iPad, a summary graphic can be created during the session that can be combined with a photo of the speaker, the title of the talk and a very brief summary of key points from the talk.

— Diane Durand, Discovery Doodles

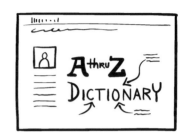

Time Lapse Video

With the magic of video editing, a video can be created that gives an overview of the event from start to finish, with graphic scribing of key points and snippets of the speakers themselves via iPad. Check out "TEDx Copenhagen 2012 Big Picture Speeddrawing" on YouTube for a great example.

— Ole Qvist-Sørensen, Bigger Picture, Denmark

Graphically Designed Summary Report

Using the skills of a graphic designer, a report can be created that really engages a participant as well as someone who was not at the event using notes, highlights and annotations of the presentations, along with quotes for reflection and spot graphics from charts that were created. Using a very visual format and professional writers, the summary can provide a great

way to educate people on what happened during the event. Check out www. crockerartmuseum.org, scroll down and click on "Pushing Our Practice with Museum Thought Leaders" to see a great example.

— Emily Shepard, The Graphic Distillery

Emails with References to Event and Relevant Articles

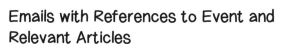

Even after the *Wisdom 2.0 Conference* concluded, emails continued to arrive that included thoughtful quotes from keynote speakers, links to articles related to conference topics and links to video from the event. Many of the same things were also on the conference Facebook page, with photos from the event. These all served as ways to continue the learning, and many comments from participants continued the participant networking.

— Dana Wright, Take Action Inc.

BEST PRACTICES: The Rule of Seven

The Rule of Seven

Touch your people seven times with the big ideas and messages of the meeting. Whatever your driving intent for the meeting, whatever the ideas you want them to take away, find ways to reach back out after the meeting and share the information again. You can reach out with film clips, digitized

visuals, have your attendees tell the story, a quick email immediately after the meeting, easy viral edutainment stuff like cartoons, and send them home with a visual template to share. The last thing you can do in your seven touches is to invite your people to take the meeting to the next level and start creating next steps and questions to bring back for another meeting.

— Janine Underhill, Founder and CEO of Idea 360 – The Art of Possibility and Amplify the Impact

Graphic Placemats

You can take a graphic printed up in 11x17 format, have it laminated and distributed as placemats to the participants . . . or print the graphics on coffee mugs.

— Avril Orloff, Outside the Lines

Chapter 10: Meeting Basics

It was an amazing event, in a beautiful setting in Washington, DC. I was one of six graphic facilitators and we had a monumental task ahead: to each create a single graphic from six futurist speakers who would be rotating through six breakout rooms. We wanted the charts to look enough alike, but not identical. We were trying to create a unique experience for each small group. What actually happened? Nothing like we wanted. As frequently happens, the participants in my group know each other, but I didn't know anyone. I struggle to remember each name as they introduce themselves, but I was not successful. They sat in a circle, but tables are between themselves and the chart. If that weren't enough, there was no one facilitating the thought leader conversations, so off it goes. I was wishing that people were wearing name tags so I could refer to them by name, or that at least someone was managing the conversation.

Brian Camastral, CEO of Riversong Sanctuary, Cofounder of BLITS Foundations, and former Global President of a large CPG company, talks about putting these basics together as choreography. "I always spend a ton of time on the choreography. Choreography to me plays a role in design thinking to create inspiring meeting spaces, better energy management, and varied interactions to stimulate, create dialogue, synthesize, re-energize, and accommodate both introverts and extroverts in their own ways. Sometimes people work better by themselves, sometimes in small groups, and sometimes in larger groups."

Design of the meeting, as we now know, makes a huge difference. How you use time and space, but how you create the details to stimulate your participants and help them reach their goals and take from the meeting those key ideas you want them to remember is alchemy. Nothing should be left to chance. There are opportunities everywhere to reinforce learning and connection.

Sometimes it's incredible to notice what we take for granted! Here are some very simple ideas for what can be changed to ensure a bigger impact on the participants' experience.

NAME TAGS YOU CAN READ

Ever been to a meeting where the purpose was meeting new people and networking, yet the name tags were obviously printed by someone who had never attended a conference? The type is so small you would need to read it like a book. That is not a networking opportunity, that is eyestrain.

And while we're at it, let's give some thought to having those impossible-to-read name tags land in a place that's not awkward to be staring at, right ladies? And not damage our clothes. And while we're at it, maybe even be recyclable or reusable?

The perfect name tag is big—HUGE—enough to read the person's first name, at a bare minimum. Then you can get creative and find other ways to make that tag support your goals and the goals of your participants, perhaps including where they're from or their favorite destination—something that can spark a conversation amongst strangers.

CONVERSATIONAL SEATING

How about as you look through the conference brochure, scoping out all the incredible workshops you want to attend, and you get to the room and note that it's set up like your third grade classroom, with no plan for the speaker to interact with you or others in the room, let alone for you to talk with others?

You know when you enter a room and immediately can tell whether the room is set for interaction or maximum capacity? I don't know about you, but somehow when I see rows and rows of seats, I get into a movie-watching mindset: I'm not thinking I'm participating anymore, but instead just receiving information. I go into complacent mode, which is aided by the lack of any eyeball connection with other participants. I'm my own island. Other times no tables is a good thing, allowing chairs to migrate all around the room and people to cluster, talk, and share. But stadium seating is never a great sign.

Contrast this to when I enter a room and there are round tables with playful things in the middle, things that can occupy my hands as I listen, I feel involved. I remember attending an Innovation Games workshop where, when we entered the room, each table was covered with stickers, glitter, glue, toys, and a variety of other items. We were invited to make our table-tent name banner as personal as we wished. We not only stepped up to the task as a way to get engaged, but to engage with other participants. In addition, we continued to play with these items throughout the workshop.

I have heard meeting planners say, "Well, these are the chairs they have." I don't buy that. If you are really trying to create a memorable event, nothing should be left to what the facility has on hand. I have been in many events where seating was brought in especially for the meeting. I walked by a session where high-tech developers were working, and the room was filled with white leather couches (not sure I would have chosen white). For another meeting I worked on, we brought in colorful couches, coffee tables, plants, and even small vases of flowers. In yet another, there were round couch "pod" set-ups with electronic whiteboards to replace flip chart stands. Another event, a two-day strategy session, used only red bean bags, which were easy to drag to various locations in the room for breakout sessions. The point I'm trying to make is this: with good planning, you can set up the space so it supports your objectives.

I was recently leading a facilitation skills workshop, and a participant asked me if there was any research on using toys. My answer: why yes there is. Research has shown that having something in your hand while listening helps many people's brains create connections. Just resist the urge to throw balls at other participants. And of course, don't throw them at the facilitator.

PROFESSIONAL FACILITATION

I've been asked many times: Why do people hire you to facilitate meetings? What's the advantage of having someone whose sole job is to facilitate a group? To me, the answer is simple. Hiring an external person ensures that every attendee can participate in the conversation, since there's someone whose job is to focus on initiating and facilitating the conversations.

When I facilitate groups, I know I'm responsible for getting the participants to their outcomes, whether it's a decision, a list of actions, or even just a productive conversation where everyone has an equal voice in the room. Many people think this will magically happen, but when you have a limited time together and lots to accomplish, isn't it better to have someone you can hold accountable for doing just that? One of my favorite quotes from a friend: "Do what you do best and hire the rest." I don't try to do my own dental work, why should a leader try to facilitate a conference?

Think back on how much of the meeting or event's success depends on your goals and outcomes and the goals of your participants. It's a great idea to have an expert help you create a plan that will get you there and then make it happen.

Leaders and planners often worry about the cost of professional facilitation. Lenny Lind, Founder and Chairman of CoVision, says, "This does come up with my clients," and still, "it's a fairly big step to go from no facilitator designer to facilitator designer." He says professional facilitation "has a cost. On the other hand you've got 150 of your leaders together for two days, I mean how much have you spent? Before we even start talking about opportunity cost and them away from their jobs for a couple of days, it's hundreds and hundreds and thousands of dollars and so, if ours is a bit more, what's the big deal?" His point? You have spent a ton of money to make this happen, you should want to ensure it happens right.

MODERN TECHNOLOGY

If you're trying to create engagement with a Twitter #hashtag, a mobile app, and a Facebook page for your event, then you MUST make sure the conference center provides enough internet capacity to handle the number of people coming to the event. It would also be prudent to have someone on the team that can troubleshoot problems with both connections

and social media sites. There will be tech problems. There are *always* tech problems.

All that said, technology can be wonderful. Using iPads, you can upload the graphic charts from the speakers and sessions, welcoming discussion through blogs, Twitter, Facebook, and other websites. You can be green and collect all the handouts and slide decks on jump drives, on the Internet, on a website, or though a mobile app. All of these give your participants something to do with their need to use social media on-the-go that is productive and engaged.

In fact, working with technology, and not against it, is such a hot topic in meetings that Chapter 12 is dedicated to just that topic.

FOOD

Sugar rush and sugar blues are not a way to go through the day. Try feeding your participants in ways that give them sustained energy. Try using the food at your event to highlight the themes or objectives of the event.

Brian Camastral found food and health so important that he brought in an health expert in to create nutritious meals and to speak at the conference. In addition, he worked with his leaders on stress reduction and creating community. He said at first his people begged him not to do this, especially the yoga, but in the end "it's the only time in my career where I remember people telling me they were leaving the meeting with more energy than they had when they arrived at the meeting."

TIME AND SPACE

Build in time for people to network. Creating spaces for hanging out allows people to process the information, connect it with things they already know. It also allows them to talk, discuss, and learn from others who have heard the information through a different lens and therefore attach a different meaning to it.

We also know that extroverts and introverts have very different ways of processing information. Extroverts get energy from being around others, which introverts find to be draining. Introverts in particular need downtime so they can recharge their bodies and their minds. They need processing time.

SUMMARY

The details of your event matter. Things like name tags, seating arrangements, use of technology, having a professional facilitator, the food you serve, and the time you create for networking and thinking all go into achieving your goals for your event. The better you can use these tools the more engagement you will have and the better the experience for your participants.

Chapter 11: Cutting-Edge Yet Low-Tech Ideas

Early in my career, I attended an industry conference in the beautiful hills of Sonoma. On the agenda, I saw something called "World Café." I was in a room full of very experienced meeting facilitators who seemed to know what they were doing. As a group, we were sent out to small tables covered in white paper, with a small vase containing two flowers, and three to four colored markers—picture what an outdoor café might look like in Paris or Vienna.

Once seated, we were given a question to discuss at our tables and were encouraged to talk and write our thoughts and ideas on the paper. After a while, we were asked to select someone to stay at the table (the host), while the rest of us scattered to other tables (not together) where the hosts shared what the previous group had talked about. We were then given a second question to discuss. The conversations were fascinating and modeled after the way conversations often happen in a bar or café.

GREAT IDEAS YOU CAN USE NOW

I've come across many, many low-tech processes used in meetings that help people network and share thoughts, ideas, and Best Practices. Some have been around for a long time, while others have been invented by Millennials who are tired of the same old, same old that traditional conferences offer. Here are a handful of these practices, with descriptions of

how they work and the benefits of each. In some cases, there may be whole books devoted to the practice.

BOF (Birds of a Feather)

Birds of a Feather are informal discussion groups formed in an ad-hoc manner. The acronym was coined by the Internet Engineering Task Force. A BOF session is an informal meeting at conferences where the attendees group together based on a shared interest and carry out discussions without any pre-planned agenda. Sometimes these are called SIG's (special interest groups).

BOFs can be a great way to get participants networking among subgroups, functionally oriented groups (e.g., CEOs), or geographically oriented groups. Though they are not formal, there is usually an appointed discussion leader and there can be a topic or agenda that is decided by the group.

Fishbowl

In this format, a small group of people discuss an issue or question while the remainder of the group listens to the conversation. When the smaller fishbowl—called the fishbowl because everyone is on the outside looking and listening—is a group of experts, they may relish the idea

of asking questions and debating with other presenters. A facilitator can also get the conversation started by asking a question of them. This can be done with just participants as well. As people who aren't sitting on the inner circle fishbowl want to contribute, they can tap someone on the shoulder who is sitting on the inner circle, who will then relinquish their chair.

Lightning Talks

Lightning talks are short presentations given at a conference or similar forums. Formats vary between venues. Most conferences will assign a speaking slot (thirty to ninety minutes) and arrange several talks one after the other during a session. The length of talks are usually between one and ten minutes with a five-minute limit being common. In order to allow rapid changes between speakers, slides may either be discouraged or a single computer running the presentation is shared by all speakers.

Narrative Therapy

Adapted from therapy, the concept helps in "thickening" the dialogue between a panel of experts and the audience. The process begins with panelists responding to three questions (telling). The audience is then invited to reflect and respond to what has been said, using their own life experiences and connection to what was said; in some cases, an image may be evoked from the discussion. Next, the panelists comment on what they heard or felt during the participant dialogue and then, as a last go-round, the audience

is again invited to comment on the panel discussion. This iterative method really allows a deep conversation between presenters and participants.

Open Space Technology

Open Space is a self-organizing method of quickly creating as many sessions as participants have passion for and want to talk about. The format/method was developed by Harrison Owen in the mid-1980s and has been rediscovered by a new generation of event organizers. The agenda is created by the attendees at the beginning of the meeting. Anyone who wants to initiate a discussion on a topic can claim a time and a space. Often it simply involves having a stack of blank paper or super-sized sticky notes; then people write topics to discuss and post them around. "Vote with your feet" is one of the core tenets, so you go where you have energy and feel you can add value. "The right people will show up" is another tenet. Participants are encouraged to move on to other groups when they're not teaching, learning, or otherwise getting or adding value.

Pecha Kucha

This is the way to have speakers do twenty slides, each for only twenty seconds. Each gathering consists of a short five-minute presentation followed by twenty minutes of table talk. Then, the group moves on to the next

topic. Pecha Kucha is a way to control the haze that comes from too much PowerPoint and a way to capture the energy of quick information followed by discussion.

Presenter Discussion Groups

At an event, after three to four presenters complete their talks, they go to four separate corners of the room, where each has a dedicated graphic recorder to capture the conversation. Participants are broken up into smaller groups and moved to one of the four corners, where the presenter engages them in a more intimate conversation about the topic, as well as solicits questions to answer. The groups rotate after a while so each person has a more personal encounter with the speaker. This certainly allows topics and questions to surface that would not have come up in the larger group. With graphic recording, the conversations can be seen by the entire group.

An even simpler version of this is used by colleague, John Williams. After each presentation, he asks the group to quickly share their Key Takeaways or Key Messages, which are graphically captured. This technique allows people to assess what they heard and hear from others.

Speed Dating

While traditionally used for meeting a potential romantic partner, the concepts of speed dating can be applied to conferences as a way to network.

In fact, Silicon Valley employs these concepts at events so entrepreneurs can meet potential investors. Using coded name tags or structured, timed rounds with introductory questions, people can meet others who can help them, provide or give information, or just learn about something they don't know about.

Speed Geeking

Using a large room, all presenters are arranged in a big circle along the edge of the room. The remaining members of the audience stand at the center of the room. Ideally there are about six to seven audience members for each presenter. One person acts as the facilitator and rings a bell to start. Presenters have a short duration, usually five minutes, to give their presentation and answer questions to small groups. Often, they are allowed to use flip chart-sized boards as visual aids. At the end of the five minutes, the facilitator rings a bell. At this point, each group moves over to the presenter to their right and the timer starts once more. The session ends when every group has attended all the presentations.

TED-Format Talks

TED Talks—TED stands for Technology, Education, and Design—have had a big impact on mainstream presentations and are spreading into the way they're structured. Considered Short Talks, each speaker is given a

maximum of eighteen minutes to present their ideas in the most innovative and engaging ways they can. They can use slides, but many don't, opting to use other visual aids to convey their points (Bill Gates released mosquitoes from a jar to demonstrate the constant fear of malaria in Africa. The mosquitoes he released were not carrying the disease, of course). (Refer back to Chapter 6 and the 'TED Commandments.')

Unconference

An unconference is a participant-driven meeting. The term unconference has been applied, or self-applied, to a wide range of gatherings that try to avoid one or more aspects of a conventional conference, such as high fees, sponsored presentations, and top-down organizations. The topics are often organized using Open Space concepts.

World Café

These rotating small group discussions generally take around twenty to forty minutes per round. The table host is one person who stays behind and welcomes the new participants to the table. The host is not a professional facilitator or a topic expert, simply a volunteer. The

conversation can change topics or questions from round to round or stay and build on one topic or question. The small table and paper setting help to create the "café" environment. If you want a little bit of structure, Neuland (see Resources) carries printed table templates that help structure the process a little bit. Again, graphic recording can capture the summary of the discussions.

SUMMARY

There are so many ways you can create events to use the interests, knowledge, and excitement of your participants and not just professional speakers. More informal methods of information sharing can take your event away from a snooze fest and make it a place where everyone is actively participating, getting their hands dirty, and loving it. These do not need to be expensive or high-tech, they can involve the visual aspects of World Café and graphic recording or be as simple as groups finding each other because of shared needs and interests. They are also great ways to meet others and network.

Chapter 12: We've Got Lots of Technology, Let's USE It

A few years ago, I walked around a 250-person conference. I was working in Phoenix, at the same location a partner organization was holding their annual conference. I was struck by the

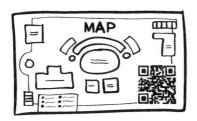

use of technology to get people oriented when there was so much going on at the same hotel. They used QR codes that were posted to give people directions to various events and more details for the day's agenda. Computers were set up to allow people to log in and post thoughts about the keynote sessions without eye and finger strain on phone keyboards. Signs with #hastags and website links were posted so people could quickly post using their phones. I wished every event could be like that.

At another conference I worked recently, people were ENCOURAGED to tweet about the various speakers and sessions they were attending. It was a form of virtual conversation that was going on between attendees. Of course, others who knew the #hashtag for the conference but were not physically present could also chime in. Twitter is old hat, everyone knows about it, but it added a level of engagement to the meeting that drew in the participants and outsiders like magic.

GOOD OR EVIL, TECHNOLOGY IS HERE

Lenny Lind, Founder and Chairman of CoVision, says that technology is "an accelerant or an inductor or a facilitator of much smaller group discussion that you would otherwise normally have in a large group meeting." Technology can be used to engage people in ways that are new and exciting.

However, it can be a way to create a Yawn Fest too, if used poorly. Lind says, "PowerPoint, as a great example, has actually made presenters worse because they rely on the technology rather than leveraging it. So, it's just created worse presentations and worse speakers."

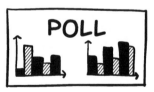

"We talk a lot about making active participants out of passive audiences."

— Lenny Lind, CoVision

There are so many unexplored possibilities for using technology, let's get to the great ones.

In 2003, I was at a meeting where Lind and his experienced team from San Francisco-based CoVision, were setting up computers—at the time, it was colorful clamshell Macintosh iBook G3s—for participants to use

for polling and online surveys to get a pulse of how people were thinking throughout the event. This was a multi-day, internal meeting of 150 senior leaders in the business. There were presentations, followed by

table polling of the group to find out their feelings about the direction and strength of each strategy.

It was early gamification in that you could see on a large screen how your table's vote compared to others. And it was much faster than lengthy report-outs, where people are happy to share their own ideas, but not so happy to listen to twelve other tables report out on the same topic.

Today, technology is readily available and is everywhere we look, yet it seems we still have mixed feelings about using it when we're in conferences. We can't figure out if we want to ban it or embrace it. I'm sure there are some generational issues that go along with this—younger attendees, as digital natives (they've never lived in a world that DIDN'T have technology), can't imagine how you WOULDN'T have technology embedded at every opportunity, and are motivated by such engagement. This young generation is certainly frustrated that cell phones, computers, and tablets are frowned upon by the more senior attendees, who would often just prefer to have them left at the door.

People of the middle generation certainly cannot put it down. They use their phones all the time, whether or not they should, and they are texting, answering email, and going on Facebook, so it might be a good idea to find a way to harness all that energy and bring it into the conference.

I have mixed feelings, to be honest. Depending on the event—both in terms of size and purpose—I could see some technologies being appropriate and others not. For example, in a smaller, company-specific event, I don't think it would be appropriate to be tweeting about the presenter's topic or the conversation. But in an industry event, I think it's great to have an online conversation about the speaker, their topic, and the impact of that topic on other issues, especially related to the conference theme.

And it's a great event when, not only those at the event attend, but others outside the event have an opportunity to participate as well. The idea of having more transparency and more open sharing as a way to build a bigger community than what can be created in an event seems like a very positive thing—it doesn't take away from the event, it actually enhances it.

Lind says technology "is the thing that facilitates making meaning out of large group process. You get the intimacy and the sharing and the knowledge and knowledge transfer and all that you have in a small group. It's there. It's current. It's right now and it's respond-able by the presenter or the leaders or whatever. You could do the whole thing manually except you never would because it would take too much time." Technology, when used right, makes the world and meetings smaller and more intimate, not the opposite.

I was working as a graphic facilitator during a senior level leadership program, and it was great to see iPads in every participant's hands. These devices had been given out as part of the program, and each had been pre-loaded with speaker PowerPoint decks, information about the other attendees, and logistics for the meeting. As graphic charts were created, they were quickly digitized and uploaded so they could be seen and referenced by everyone in the room.

LIVING EXAMPLES

Stephen Zaruba and John Quereto, Partners and Regional Practice Directors for Expressworks, an organizational change consulting firm based in San Francisco Bay Area and Houston, Texas, give a great example of using technology effectively:

"I was at a conference a couple of years ago where their agenda was an app on everybody's iPhone, and that was the coolest thing because as they made agenda changes, so they were sensitive to the flow and to where people's interest were. And so they would adjust the agenda but it was immediately then downloaded on everybody's phone and it was so cool."

Vivian Li shares how they do it: "Our facilitator, David, incorporated the 'how to' for the Think Tank tool into an icebreaker. We all

put the wildest thing we'd done and in doing so, learned how to enter data. Then we categorized the data into 'Meh,' 'Wild,' and 'OMG!' while learning how to create affinity groups. Finally, we voted on the wildest 'OMG' items, thus learning how to vote. The entire exercise took seven minutes and at the end, we had learned how to use the tool and broke the ice."

Brian Camastral, CEO of Riversong Sanctuary, Cofounder of BLITS Foundation, and former Global President of a large CPG company, talked about creating that website where everything from the conference lived: presentations, video, digitized images of graphic roadmaps, voice recordings, flip charts. People could draw from it and use the content to tell stories back at their jobs. The conference lived on virtually.

Greg Bogue, Experience Architect at Maritz Travel, uses technology up front. "One of the things that I'm part of is this whole idea of creating a content website, where you're registering and stuff, they're asking you for some of your key thoughts are big questions and those are actually being reviewed as they're creating discussion those around those ideas."

These are only a few ways in which befriending technology and inviting it into your meeting can create engagement.

SUMMARY

The bottom line is this: technology is NOT going away and can be a great way to enhance learning and create networking opportunities. Furthermore, people will come to expect it to be embedded at every touch point, so to not have it will be an oddity. Organizers and planners need to think about where it could be used to enhance learning and networking and build community.

Resources

Books

Okay, a confession.

I am a book addict. The "Hello, my name is Dana and I'm a book addict" kind. I absolutely love a good bookstore and the opportunity to touch and look through lots and lots of information. Amazon Prime is like crack cocaine, so I have a lot of great books. And I have no sponsor, so the collection grows. Some I've read cover to cover, many I've flipped through and gathered lots of great ideas. My guarantee? You will definitely find many diamonds in this list.

Agerbeck, Brandy. *The Graphic Facilitator's Guide.* Loosetooth.com. 2012.

Bergren, Mark, Molly Cox, and Jim Detmar. *Improvise This! How to Think On Your Feet So You Don't Fall On Your Face.* Hyperion. 2002.

Carlson, Curtis and William Wilmot. *Innovation: The 5 Disciplines for Creating What Customers Want.* Crown Publishing. 2006.

Chopyak, Christine. *Picture Your Business Strategy.* McGraw Hill. 2013.

Colan, Lee J. *Engaging the Hearts and Minds of All Your Employees: How to Ignite Passionate Performance for Better Business Results.* McGraw Hill. 2009.

Doyle, Michael and David Straus. *How To Make Meetings Work*. Jove Books. 1982.

Duarte, Nancy. *Resonate: Present Visual Stories That Transform Audiences*. Wiley. 2010.

Duarte, Nancy. *Slide:ology: The Art and Science of Creating Great Presentations*. O'Reilly Media. 2008.

Foster, Hayley. *Don't Tank Your TED Talk! 12 Mistakes Professional Speakers Make*. Self Published. 2013.

Gaskins, Robert. *Sweating Bullets: Notes About Inventing PowerPoint*. Vinland Books. 2012.

Gray, Dave, Sunni Brown, and James Macanufo. *Gamestorming: A Playbook for Innovators, Rulebreakers, and Changemakers*. O'Reilly Media. 2010.

Heath, Chip and Daniel Heath. *Made to Stick: Why Some Ideas Survive and Others Die*. Random House. 2007.

Hohmann, Luke. *Innovation Games*. Addison-Wesley Professional. 2006.

Johansen, Bob. *Get There Early: Sensing the Future to Compete in the Present*. Barrett Kohler. 2007.

Kaner, Sam. *Facilitator's Guide to Participatory Decision-Making.* Jossey-Bass. 2007.

Lawrence, Paul R. and Nitin Nohria. *Driven.* Jossey-Bass. 2002.

LeFever, Lee. *The Art of Explanation: Making Your Ideas, Products, and Services Easier to Understand.* Wiley. 2012.

Liteman, Merianne, Sheila Campbell, and Jeff Liteman. *Retreats That Work: Everything You Need to Know About Planning and Leading Great Offsites.* Wiley. 2006.

Margolis, Michael. *Believe Me: A Storytelling Manifesto for Change-Makers and Innovators.* Get Storied Press. 2009.

Margulies, Nancy and Christine Valenza. *Visual Thinking: Tools for Mapping Your Ideas.* Crown House Publishing. 2005.

Osterwalder. Alexander and Yves Pigneur. *Business Model Generation: A Handbook for Visionaries, Game Changers, and Challengers.* Wiley. 2010.

Paharia, Rajat. *Loyalty 3.0: How to Revolutionize Customer and Employee Engagement with Big Data and Gamification.* McGraw Hill. 2013.

Pink, Daniel. *A Whole New Mind: Why Right Brainers Will Rule the Future.* Penguin Press. 2006.

Petz, Jon. *Boring Meetings Suck*. Wiley. 2011.

Roam, Dan. *Back of the Napkin: Solving Problems and Selling Ideas With Pictures (Expanded Edition)*. Portfolio Trade. 2013.

Roam, Dan. *Blah Blah Blah: What To Do When Words Don't Work*. Portfolio Hardcover. 2011.

Rohde, Mike. *The Sketchnote Handbook: The Illustrated Guide to Visual Note Taking*. Peachpit Press. 2012.

Segar, Adrian. *Conferences That Work: Creating Events That People Love*. Booklocker.com. 2010.

Sibbet, David. *Visual Meetings: How Graphics, Sticky Notes and Idea Mapping Can Transform Group Productivity*. Wiley. 2010.

Sinek, Simon. *Start With Why: How Great Leaders Inspire Everyone to Take Action*. Portfolio Trade. 2011.

Spencer, Laura. *Winning Through Participation*. Kendall/Hunt Publishing. 1989.

Surowiecki, James. *The Wisdom of Crowds*. Anchor Books. 2005.

Tomorrow Makers, Inc. *"Events by Design: Facilitating Through the 7 Domains."* PDF download.

World Café Community, et al. *The World Café: Shaping Our Futures Through Conversations That Matter.* Berrett-Koehler Publishers. 2005.

Resources and Tools

Increasingly, hotels don't have wall space to accommodate large wall graphics; however, you can make your own wall space using common items. Sometimes you may put paper over these four-foot by eight-foot boards, and other times you may choose to draw right on them and display them. Here are a few resources:

- Foam Insulation Board

  - This can be found at Home Depot and Lowes; you want to get a minimum thickness of 1" (2" is better) so they are sturdy and don't flex as you draw on them. They are not expensive at all; if you need to fold them, score them on one side and fold (don't cut all the way through!)

- Cinec PVC Board
  - I just learned about this material, but PVC would be a great, smooth surface to write on.

- Biodegradable Foamboard
  - Although more expensive than traditional foam core, The Gilman Brothers Company makes environmentally responsible foamboards for meetings and events. They are available around the world.
  - www.gilmanbrothers.com

And here are some other great resources:

- Bunchball
  - As a leader in gamification, Bunchball knows what motivates people to take action: a goal that matters, recognition among peers, and a meaningful reward. Bunchball Nitro puts the most advanced gamification engine to work for you—combining what you know about your audience with proven motivation techniques to achieve real results.
  - www.bunchball.com

- Catch Box
  - A soft wireless microphone that you can throw into audiences to kickstart a discussion, turn large Q&A into seamless discussion and give smaller group meetings structure. (Not available yet—check out their site to see the concept.)
  - www.thecatchbox.com

- Command Strips
  - A 3M product that allows you to attach foamboards to a wall, without any damage.
  - www.command.com

- The Grove Consultants International
  - The Grove sell a great selection of meeting supplies, including tape, markers, large paper, guides and meeting templates.
  - www.grove.com

- IdeaPaint
  - This is a dry erase paint that turns virtually any surface into an erasable canvas, giving you the space you need to collaborate, interact and fully explore your creativity.
  - www.ideapaint.com

- Neuland Refillable Markers and Meeting Supplies
  - My colleague Guido Neuland has an incredible selection of meeting supplies; most notable are portable walls that can be set up anywhere and his amazing collection of refillable colored markers in various sizes.
  - www.neuland.com

- Tagxedo (also Wordle)
  - Turns words—famous speeches, news articles, slogans and themes, even your love letters—into a visually stunning word cloud, words individually sized appropriately to highlight the frequencies of occurrence within the body of text.
  - www.tagxedo.com

- Visual Explorer Cards
  - These decks of cards contain 216 images of an amazing array of situations. The tool provides a method for supporting collaborative, creative conversations in a wide variety of situations to help develop ideas and insights into useful dialogue. I find the best size to work with groups is the postcard size.
  - http://solutions.ccl.org

- Wizard Wall
  - A cling film that turns any indoor surface into an easel without the need for tape, pins, or nails.
  - www.wizardwall.com

- Wizer
  - By giving every individual a voice, wizerizing turns attendees into active participants and accelerates knowledge sharing, learning and co-creation.
  - www.wizerize.com

ACKNOWLEDGMENTS

This amazing collection of thoughts, ideas, quotes, and best practices was an incredible demonstration of collaboration and my belief in community. I am so delighted to have had conversations with some of the best: Greg Bogue, Brian Camastral, Nancy Duarte, Hayley Foster, Lenny Lind, John Quereto, David Sibbet, Gail Taylor, and Stephen Zaruba.

The Best Practices was a shared labor of love, done by both telephone and email networking, often using Facebook for sources. Thank you to my talented and innovative colleagues who spent time with me on the phone: Lisa Arora, Diane Durand, Nevada Lane, Sophia Liang, Sita Magnuson, Avril Orloff, Emily Shepard, Julie Stuart, Janine Underhill, and Anthony Weeks. Thank you to the many others who agreed, often without knowing anything more about me than my profession, to let me publish their ideas and trust I would credit them. Spread out across the globe, I hope to someday meet you and thank you personally.

Many thanks to the earliest readers of what was not really a book, but more a concept, and strongly encouraged me to continue nonetheless: Sam Horn—who gave me the brilliant title and said I was onto something and to keep going, Lisa Arora—who both cheered me on when I was fired up and cheered me up when I was struggling, Geoff Ball—who said I had really stimulated his thinking about the subject, Jesse Fewell—who said what I was writing was so much more than a book, and Vivian Li—who tirelessly accepted my requests for feedback and input, day and night.

So many others agreed to give guidance, encouragement, and input along the way—some clients and others colleagues, all people I would call friends: Elaine Allison, Charles Anderson, Denise Brosseau, Franziska Bussiek, Cari Caldwell, Renee Gellatly, Tami Majer, Christina Merkley, Kristina Richter, Jen Schulte, Kathy Waite and Trish Wynot. And a special thank you to my long-time friend Matthew Ajiake, who always encourages me and quickly provided the ISBN number I needed. Deidre Fuller took the beautiful picture that appears on the back (how I wish I always looked that pulled together) and Prakash Patodia took every interview file I sent him in India and turned it into something readable and quotable. And to Josh and Paola at my FedEx Kinko's in Campbell, thank you for always greeting me with a smile and encouragement.

The inspiration for the format of this book goes to Alexander Osterwalder and Yves Pigneur, whose book *Business Model Generation* inspired me to not only collaborate with colleagues near and far, but stick to my dream of making a very visual book.

I consider myself to be beyond lucky to have put together the most amazing team to help me midwife this book into existence. This includes:

- Michelle Auerbach, who not only served as a fantastic editor, but a great project manager, coach, and cheerleader when I was feeling like I wasn't going to make it.
- Julia Restin, who wandered into my life just out of college and suddenly found herself at ground zero, pulling the various pieces of this book together, from release edits to illustrations to layout challenges. She handled each challenge with amazing grace and patience.
- Marianne Rodgers, who is the yin to my yang in terms of graphics and layout. We have a symbiotic respect for what the other does and her ability to sort out my thoughts and put them into a beautiful format is truly an amazing talent.
- Nate Tanemori, who I found at just the right moment on Craigslist of all places. He immediately understood my need for a visual book at our very first meeting and was a true professional throughout the process. He was willing to challenge my thinking about layout and helped me *really* see how things could be better.
- Emily Shepard, who I begged to draw for the center image of the book so I could have a piece of her talent with me at all times.
- Carolyn Oakley, who jumped in at the last-minute to lend her expertise to final edits, layout tweaks, and keeping the gods of print and ebooks happy.

Finally, I would be remiss in not thanking the people who tolerate my craziness daily as I follow my passion. To my mom and dad, and sisters Caroline and Kristin, who still don't really understand what the heck it is I do, but support me nonetheless. To my beautiful and smart daughters, Kylah and Allie, I hope I model the importance of following your dreams and making things happen in the world.

WORKS CITED

CHAPTER 1

Lenny Lind (Founder and Chairman of CoVision), in discussion with the author, 2013.

David Rock, "Rethinking How We 'Conference,'" *Your Brain at Work* (blog), *Psychology Today*, April 22, 2011, http://www.psychologytoday.com/blog/your-brain-work/201104/rethinking-how-we-conference.

Meeting Professionals International; Show Me the Value; Website.

CHAPTER 2

Simon Sinek, unpublished keynote address, 2011.

Simon Sinek, *Start With Why*, Penguin, 2011.

Meetup; Website.

Robert Putnam, *Bowling Alone*, Simon & Schuster, 2001.

Iris Firstenberg, "Customer Centricity Workshop," unpublished transcript.

Tony Schwartz, *Take Back Your Attention* (blog), *Harvard Business Review*, February, 2011, http://blogs.hbr.org/schwartz/2011/02/take-back-your-attention.html.

Peter Bregman, *How (and Why) to Stop Multitasking* (blog), *Harvard Business Review*, May, 2010. http://blogs.hbr.org/bregman/2010/05/how-and-why-to-stop-multitaski.html.

CHAPTER 3

Brian Camastral (CEO Riversong Sanctuary, Cofounder BLITS Foundation, and former Global President of a large CPG company), in discussion with the author, 2013.

Steven Covey, *The Seven Habits of Highly Effective People*, Free Press, 2004.

Luc Gallopin, *Know, Feel, Do* (blog) quoting Bill Jensen of The Jensen Group, http://www.reply-mc.com/2008/12/28/know-feel-do-bottom-line-of-communication/.

Greg Bogue (Experience Architect, Maritz Travel), in discussion with the author, 2013.

Walter Isaacson, *Steve Jobs*, Simon & Schuster, 2011.

John Medina, *Brain Rules*, Pear Press, 2009.

Janine Underhill (Founder and CEO of Idea 360 – The Art of Possibility and Amplify the Impact), in discussion with the author, 2013.

Bartle Test of Gamer Psychology, gamerDNA; Website.

Paul Lawrence and Nitin Nohria, *Driven: How Human Nature Shapes Our Choices*, Jossey-Bass, 2002.

Josh Kaufman, *The Personal MBA: Master the Art of Business*, Portfolio Trade, 2012.

Rajat Paharia, *Loyalty 3.0: How to Revolutionize Customer and Employee Engagement with Big Data and Gamification*, McGraw-Hill, 2013.

Thom Singer, *Hallway Networking Is a Key Part of Conference Learning* (blog), *Some Assembly Required*, February 2012, http://thomsinger.blogspot.com/2012/02/hallway-networking-is-key-part-of.html.

Mitch Holt, *5 Benefits of Coworking* (blog), *Volacci*, December 2011, http://www.volacci.com/blog/mitch-holt/2011/december/07/5-benefits-coworking.

CHAPTER 4

Hayley Foster (Short Talk Expert and author of *Don't Tank Your TED Talk*), in discussion with the author, 2013.

Stephen Zaruba and John Quereto (Partners of change management consulting firm, Expressworks), in discussion with the author, 2013.

Peter Block, *Community: The Structure of Belonging*, Berrett-Koehler Publishers, 2009.

CHAPTER 6

Greg Bogue (Experience Architect, Maritz Travel), in discussion with the author, 2013.

Gail Taylor (Co-founder of MGTaylor Corporation and Founder and Chairman of Tomorrow Makers), in discussion with the author, 2013.

Hayley Foster (Short Talk Expert and author of *Don't Tank Your TED Talk*), in discussion with the author, 2013.

Nancy Duarte (Principal of Duarte Design), in discussion with the author, 2013.

Nancy Duarte, *Resonate: Present Visual Stories that Transform Audiences*, Wiley, 2010.

TED Commandments; Tedexoverlake; Website.

Daniel Pink, *3 tips for TED speakers (and other talkers)* (blog), *Personal Productivity*, http://www.danpink.com/2012/03/3-tips-for-ted-speakers/.

Michelle Auerbach (Organizational Storytelling Consultant, Modaka Consulting), in discussion with the author, 2013.

Anthony Weeks (Graphic Recorder), in discussion with the author, 2013.

Bon Johansen, *Get There Early*, Berrett-Koehler, 2007.

Willie Pietersen, *Strategic Learning: How to Be Smarter Than Your Competition and Turn Key Insights into Competitive Advantage*, Wiley, 2010.

David Kolb, *Kolb's Learning Styles and Experiential Learning Model*, Big Dog and Little Dog's Bowl of Biscuits; Website.

CHAPTER 8

Greg Bogue (Experience Architect, Maritz Travel), in discussion with the author, 2013.

Avril Orloff (Outside the Lines), in discussion with the author, 2013.

Janine Underhill (Founder and CEO of Idea 360 – The Art of Possibility and Amplify the Impact), in discussion with the author, 2013.

Daniel Pink, *Drive*, Riverhead Books, 2011.

Brian Camastral (CEO Riversong Sanctuary, Cofounder BLITS Foundation, and former Global President of a large CPG company), in discussion with the author, 2013.

Gail Taylor (Co-founder of MGTaylor Corporation and Founder and Chairman of Tomorrow Makers), in discussion with the author, 2013.

Chapter 10

Brian Camastral (CEO Riversong Sanctuary, Cofounder BLITS Foundation, and former Global President of a large CPG company), in discussion with the author, 2013.

Lenny Lind (Founder and Chairman of CoVision), in discussion with the author, 2013.

Brian Camastral (CEO Riversong Sanctuary, Cofounder BLITS Foundation, and former Global President of a large CPG company), in discussion with the author, 2013.

Chapter 12

Lenny Lind (Founder and Chairman of CoVision), in discussion with the author, 2013.

Stephen Zaruba and John Quereto (Partners of change management consulting firm, Expressworks), in discussion with the author, 2013.

Brian Camastral (CEO Riversong Sanctuary, Cofounder BLITS Foundation, and former Global President of a large CPG company), in discussion with the author, 2013.

Greg Bogue (Experience Architect, Maritz Travel), in discussion with the author, 2013.

You read the book. You are ready to START Meeting Like This.

We'd like to help!

We are a collection of
visual thinkers, facilitators,
process consultants, and design thinkers.

We provide services to clients, putting together one-day to multi-day events.

We partner with clients in various phases of the conference, from pre-conference preparation to post-conference follow-up to a variety of during the event offerings to support you in getting the most effective results.

We provide that WOW factor for your attendees using various visual mediums and the latest and best of organization development and facilitation.

Get in touch, talk to us about your event,
and see how you can make a difference.

www.startmeetinglikethis.com

Made in the USA
San Bernardino, CA
02 December 2016